'CAVALCADE'

This cavalcade of grace now stands,
It speaks in silence
Its story is the story of this land.
Where in this wide world can man find,
Nobility without pride, friendship without envy
Or beauty without vanity?
Here, where grace is laced with muscle,
and strength by gentleness confined,
he serves without servility; he has fought without enmity.
There is nothing so powerful,
nothing less violent; there is nothing so quick,
nothing more patient.
England's past has been borne on his back,
All our history in his industry:
We are his heirs, he our inheritance,
He is of course, the Horse.

THIS POEM IS ATTRIBUTED TO ROBERT DUNCAN AND WAS FIRST USED AT
THE HORSE OF THE YEAR SHOW IN LONDON IN 1954

For Linda
who loves horses

Royal Salute is published by:

The Royal Horse Artillery Association
King George VI Lines
Repository Road
Woolwich
London SE18 4BB

© 2012 W. G. Clarke

British Library Cataloguing in Publication Data.
A catalogue record for this book is available from the British Library.

ISBN 978-0-9520762-4-7

Designed and Produced by Paul G. Harding
Editor and Publishing Consultant: Barbara Cooper

Printed in Italy

ROYAL SALUTE

W. G. Clarke

Foreword

by The Duke of Richmond and Gordon

This book tells the story of the history, traditions and culture of the saluting battery of Her Majesty's Household Troops and its barracks at St. John's Wood. Both the role of the saluting battery and the military occupation of the barracks began in rather haphazard circumstances: which appears to have been fairly common in the relationship between Britain and its Army over the past 300 years. By the turn of the nineteenth century, both the barracks and the saluting battery had become firmly established at the heart of State ceremonial, thereby further embellishing the professional reputation of the Royal Horse Artillery in peace as well as war. I am sure this would have pleased my illustrious ancestor, Charles, 3rd Duke of Richmond, who was instrumental in the formation, organisation and training of the first troops of the Royal Horse Artillery at Goodwood in 1793.

It is indeed sad that the King's Troop, as the last horsed saluting battery to be stationed at St John's Wood, has now moved to Woolwich. Those readers who live or work in the capital will no longer be able to enjoy the morning spectacle of the Troop exercising or going about their business on the streets of London each day. It is therefore fitting that in producing this book Major Clarke has provided a unique and lasting record to celebrate a regiment, a role and a barracks which have been at the centre of London life for more than 130 years. It will also be a reminder to all who read it of the fortitude and professionalism of those members of the Royal Horse Artillery, and their horses, who served at 'The Wood' from the arrival of the first battery in 1880.

Richmond and Gordon

Introduction

The discharge of cannon as a form of salute to express joy or celebration is almost as old as artillery itself. It was certainly in vogue by the 15th century, and ever since then gun salutes have been fired to mark important occasions. Formal regulations for the marking of Royal Anniversaries and State occasions are, however relatively modern:

In fact, no military regulations existed until 1827 when the Board of Ordnance ordered that 41 guns was the correct Royal Salute when fired from St. James's Park or the Tower of London.

It was not until the early 1880s that a battery was stationed at St. John's Wood charged with responsibility for the firing of Royal Salutes on State occasions. Even at this point in history it was not unusual for the duty to be carried out by a battery from Aldershot or Woolwich. By 1902 the ceremonial role of the battery at St. John's Wood had become a firm part of its duties. In 1923 Hyde Park was the primary saluting base for the firing of Royal Salutes, and for the first time the RHA batteries could gallop into action in true Horse Gunner style. With only a short break of six years during World War Two, this tradition has continued without interruption, although nowadays Green Park is also used as a saluting base when required.

The culture, drills and practices formulated and carried out by successive batteries at the Wood between 1902 and 1939 were continued by the Riding Troop on its formation after World War Two, and later by the King's Troop. For draught training, this included the use of the open ground at Wormwood Scrubs and Old Oak Common as well as various aspects of Regents Park. As for the barrack routine itself, little changed in this respect until the early 1960s when National Service ended. Even then, much of the old routine and many of the traditions continued well into the 1970s. For those fortunate enough to have served at the Wood, the barracks with its quirky, much neglected and very Spartan Victorian-cum-Georgian character was unique, and held a very special place in their affections. For many it was indeed a 'home from home' and as important as the battery or troop in which they served. And of course there were the horses, without which nothing could have happened and life would have been incredibly dull. There were many great characters among them over the years and some served longer at the Wood and knew more of the many routines and drills than most of their human masters. They were without doubt much loved and valued by both soldiers and officers alike. Many a soldier shed a tear on 'casting day' when a great friend went off at the end of his or her working life to the great stable in the sky.

With the move of the saluting battery to Woolwich in February 2012, the connection between the Royal Regiment of Artillery and St. John's Wood has been finally severed. Moreover, the Regiment will have lost the last and oldest battery station, and one that holds the fondest of memories for all who served there. The 'Wood' was indeed unique and I doubt we shall ever see its like again. The Royal Salutes will continue however, and the sound of the guns in Hyde Park on State and ceremonial occasions might disturb a few slumbering ghosts of the many soldiers and horses that once served in the ancient barracks on Ordnance Hill. For the new residents of the barrack plot I am sure they will be forgiven if, in the evening half light of a damp or frosty winter's day, they believe they can hear the hollow clatter of hooves and the jingle of harness. If they do, it will be, along with the ancient riding school building, all that is left to remind us of two hundred years of military occupation of what was, at one time, St. John's Wood farm.

W. G. Clarke

Contents

Chapter One

EARLY BEGINNINGS

The departure of the King's Troop from St. John's Wood Barracks in 2012 brought to an end more than 200 years of almost continuous occupation by military units, in particular those of the Royal Regiment of Artillery. This chapter traces the history of the last battery station of the Royal Horse Artillery from occupation by the Corps of Gunner Drivers in 1804 until the arrival of A Battery A Brigade Royal Horse Artillery in 1880.

'History is a pattern of timeless moments.
So while the light fails
On a winter's afternoon in a secluded chapel,
History is now and England"
FROM *LITTLE GIDDING,* A POEM BY T. S. ELIOT 1888–1965

The 'Wood', as the barracks at St. John's Wood affectionately became known to many generations of Gunners who served there, was unlike any other barracks. Covering an area of little more than five acres, it combined an extraordinary mixture of architecture, old and new, attractive and very basic. Right in the middle of this eclectic mixture of buildings stood the wooden stables: 'The Lines'. Originally designed, it is said, for use in the Crimea, they survived two world wars and various attempts at refurbishment until they were demolished during the rebuild of the barracks in 1970. Despite the diversity of style and condition, the Wood possessed an atmosphere all of its own. There were trees of various size and age including a splendid elm in the corner of the barracks next to the Sergeants' Mess. These, the laurel bushes surrounding the outdoor manège, and the small lawn in front of the Officers' Mess, all combined to produce a mixture of bucolic serenity and old fashioned military efficiency, right in the heart of the bustling metropolis of London.

At the Wood, all ranks always worked hard, daily routine and military culture having been handed down through many generations of Horse Gunners. Of course, there were many changes over the years, especially since the introduction of the new Regular Army in the 1960s and more so since the Options for Change programme of the 1990s. Essentially however, apart from the odd adjustment to the full dress uniform, and the adoption of more modern Service Dress, the face of the saluting battery was little-changed from the pre-war days of the 1930s. Conversely, the daily routine and military culture of the barracks unfortunately suffered from the interference of modernity. The working day was no longer punctuated by the familiar trumpet call to work, stables, or duty, and the frequent parades throughout the day also largely disappeared. All gave way to a more modern and slightly relaxed system. Perhaps this was inevitable, given the dramatic changes that occurred in British society as a whole over the preceding forty years. At the beginning of the 19th Century, when St. John's Wood Farm was first identified and let as a military hiring, life was very different indeed.

A MILITARY HIRING

The first occupants of what was then St. John's Wood Farm were the Corps of Gunner Drivers in 1804. The farm was a simple Board of Ordnance hiring, used only for the purpose of quartering and stabling the Drivers and their horses. In those far off days, London was a distant metropolis; smoke-filled and congested, it barely reached what is now the Marylebone Road. The Boroughs of St. Marylebone and St. Pancras consisted of large dairy farms leased by tenants from a variety of landowners, among them the Eyres, who owned St. John's Wood (and, embodied by the Eyre Estate, are still ground landlords for much of it).

The area now occupied by Abbey Road on the west, and Avenue Road on the east, were meadows over which upwards of 300 head of cows grazed, driven back at milking time along the slope that was to become Ordnance Hill, across the eventual parade ground to what is now called Tatham Place, but was for many years a United Dairies bottling depot and distribution centre on Acacia Road. Here lay the yards, barns, ponds and milking sheds of the farm. The agricultural era, however, was drawing to a close. Already there were workings for brick-earth, clay and sand in the neighbouring fields, while in the area known as Marylebone Park and later transformed into Regents Park, there were gravel pits. The Eyre's tenant of St. John's Wood Farm, Thomas Willan, who also leased the larger

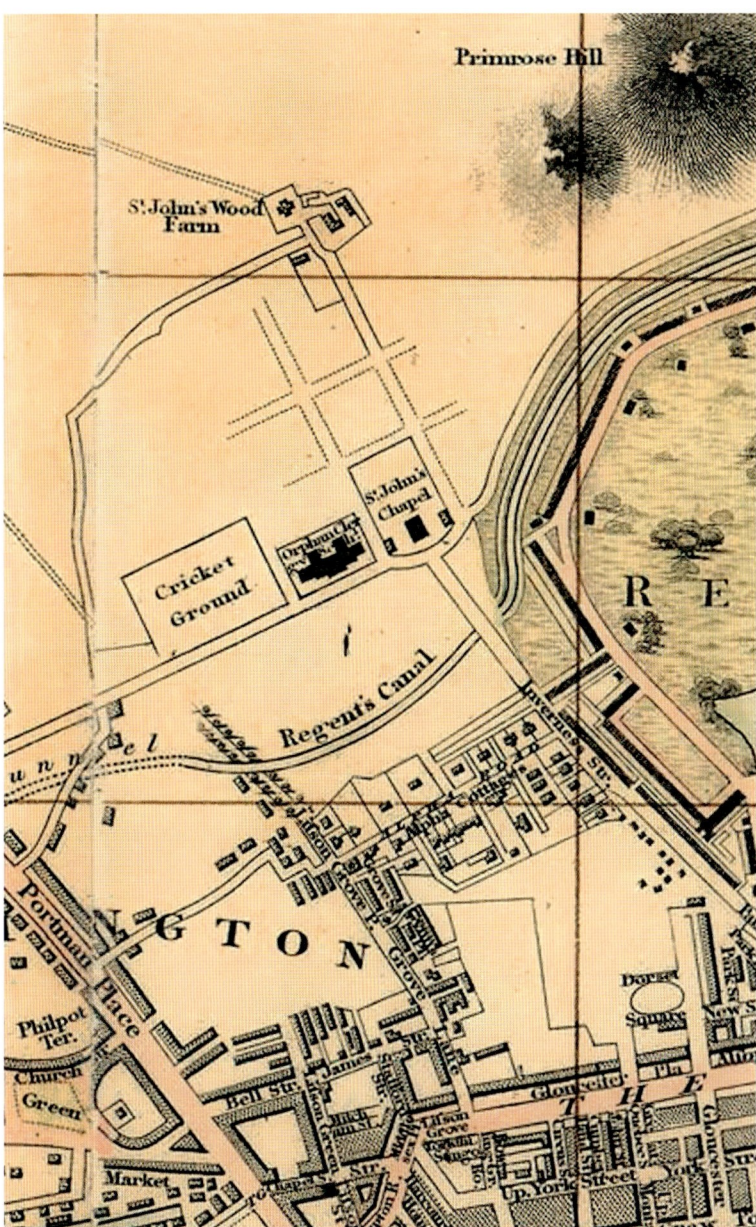

Plan view of St. John's Wood farm and the surrounding area, 1804.

Marylebone Park Farm, could, no doubt, read the signs, and perhaps it was the realisation that changes were in the air that persuaded him to lease part of the barns and outbuildings at St. John's Wood Farm to the Board of Ordnance at an annual rent of £150 a year. Thus, casually and without any hint of what would eventually rise from these small beginnings, began the Regiment's first association with St. John's Wood, although not yet with the barrack site itself.

The hiring of St. John's Wood Farm was simply routine for the Board of Ordnance. It held no special significance, although there had been talk of setting up an Ordnance Depot in Marylebone Park. No doubt the Board would have preferred to quarter the drivers more centrally, at least closer to the Brigade of Guns for which they were supposed to provide transport, for they were stationed three miles away in St. James's Park. The Corps of Gunner Drivers were a semi-independent auxiliary body. Neither its officers nor its drivers had any duties in connection with the guns. With no means of contact at that distance other than a galloper, communication must have been a problem for the commander of the Field Brigade, especially as the rationale for their very existence and location so close to Whitehall was more to do with the requirements of riot control than ceremonial duties.

A view of the Artillery Drivers barracks in 1812, with the soldiers' accommodation block on the east side of the barrack area.

Few records remain from this period to recall the relations between the soldiers and the farm workers at St. John's Wood. From one officer's mention of jobbing out horses, it is reasonable to assume that the gun teams were used for various carting jobs, especially during the haymaking season. The number of men quartered at the farm, possibly in part of the farmhouse, can be inferred from the plan which indicates a soldiers' room for 24 men and two others for 14 each. As few barracks existed at this time, and very often those that did were not built to last, the practice of billeting out officers and soldiers was common. Thus as the strength of the Corps exceeded the accommodation available, many of the officers and perhaps the senior soldiers themselves would have been billeted locally at this time. By 1810 the authorities concluded that keeping the guns and drivers so far apart was an expensive and inconvenient practice—and not conducive to military efficiency. The Board of Ordnance therefore proposed to base the whole Brigade at the farm, and to this end they secured from Mr Walpole Eyre the lease of a piece of land just north of the farmyard: the present day barrack site.

On this site the Board built a long two-storeyed barrack block, running north to south in a line roughly parallel with the present day Ordnance Hill. Designated 'New Artillery Barracks' and completed in 1812, it comprised officers' and soldiers' quarters and cost about £4,800. With low ceilings and poor ventilation it was not exactly the best start to the life of the barracks. Such married quarters as existed— six little lean-to cottages tacked onto the back of the barrack block—were little better. Here then, to this inauspicious 'barracks' came the first artillery pieces:

An early sketch of the farm in 1814.

the guns themselves being either 6-pounder or 9-pounder with perhaps the addition of a few 5½ inch howitzers. The problem of traffic control through the farmyard was solved when the Board built a 'military road' running east to west from the corner of where the Sergeants' Mess building stood to join what is now Wellington Road. During the rundown of the Army after Waterloo, the Brigade at St. John's Wood was ordered to Woolwich and not replaced. The Barracks stood empty for the next three years while the Board of Ordnance attempted to get rid of them.

As fortune would have it, by 1822 the metropolis was spreading rapidly towards the very rural village of St. John's Wood. Regents Park had been created and some of the Nash Terraces and the barracks at Albany Street, built to accommodate each Household Cavalry Regiment in turn, were in existence. Within the metropolis itself the transformation of the Buckingham House Stables into the Royal Mews was about to displace the Cavalry Riding Establishment. After much deliberation the vacant site at St. John's Wood was chosen as the new home for this establishment, and Treasury approval for the building of a new Riding School was granted. Initially estimated at £3,000, it was finally completed in 1825 at a total cost of £5,712.4s.9d. The School was designed by the Royal Engineers and the officer responsible for its completion was Brevet Major Tylden. Measuring 180 feet long by 60 feet wide, it was the largest in the London area, with eight tall, round, arched windows at each side. It is possible that when the houses were built on what is now Queen's Grove the windows on the north side were bricked up to leave only the glazed archways that exist to this day. Originally there was no clock tower—this was a later Victorian addition. Unfortunately, the Treasury

grant did not extend to the building of stables. Of the 78 horses on strength, most were stabled in a hiring about a quarter of a mile away, in what is now believed to be known as Ordnance Mews. The others were stabled in wooden buildings at the farm. The new occupants of the barracks and the farm workers lived together rather uneasily for several years: in fact until 1835, when the Cavalry Riding Establishment was moved to Maidstone. The Wood stood empty once more.

Yet again, a reorganisation of Household Troops was to bring new occupants to the Wood. On this occasion the landscaping of St. James's Park and the demolition of an untidy building, previously the home of the Guards Recruits Depot, necessitated the need for a new home for the recruits. Someone at Horse Guards with an obvious touch of genius decided that the redundant riding school at St. John's Wood could be used for drill on wet days, and the plan was adopted forthwith. To accommodate the recruits the old 1812 barracks were demolished and new housing for the soldiers was erected on the southern side of the square.

The lease for the farm and barracks, 1824.

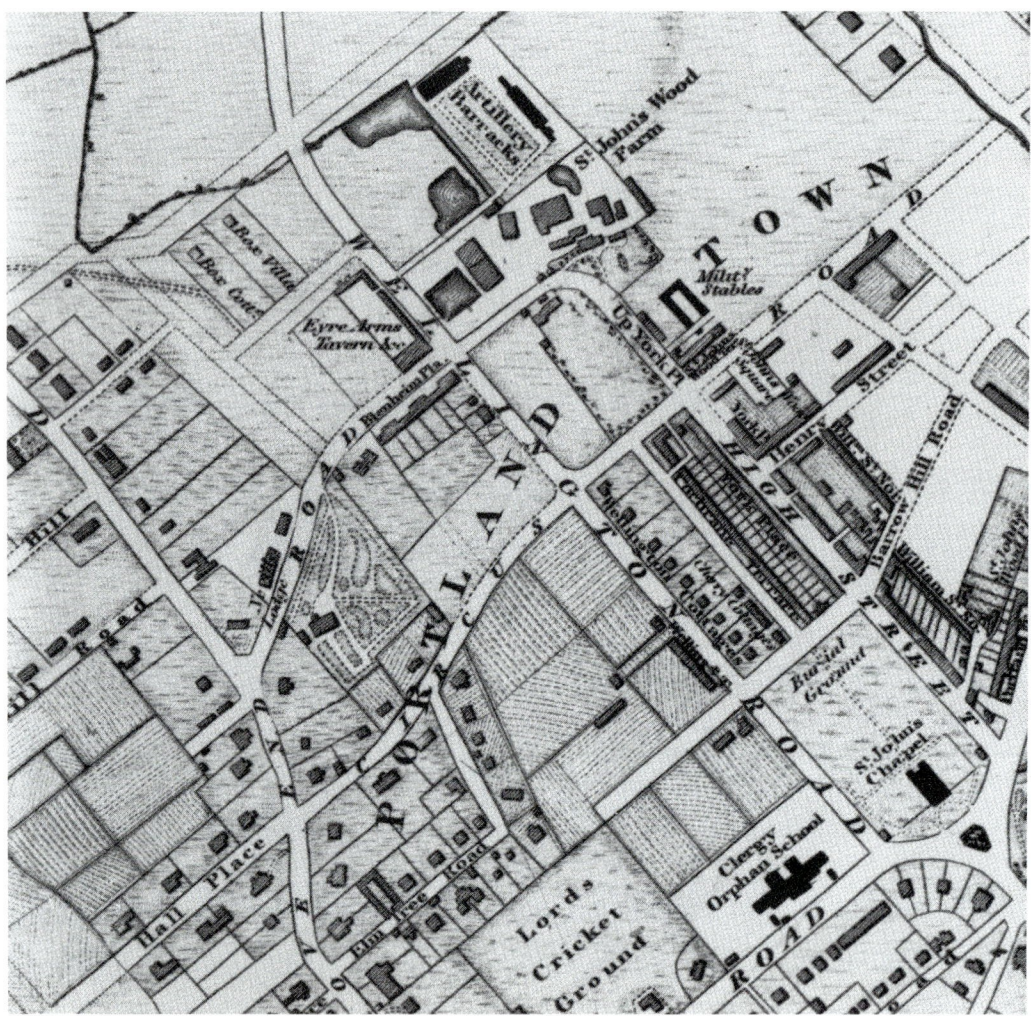

St. John's Wood 1830 with the new metropolis gradually encroaching upon the village.

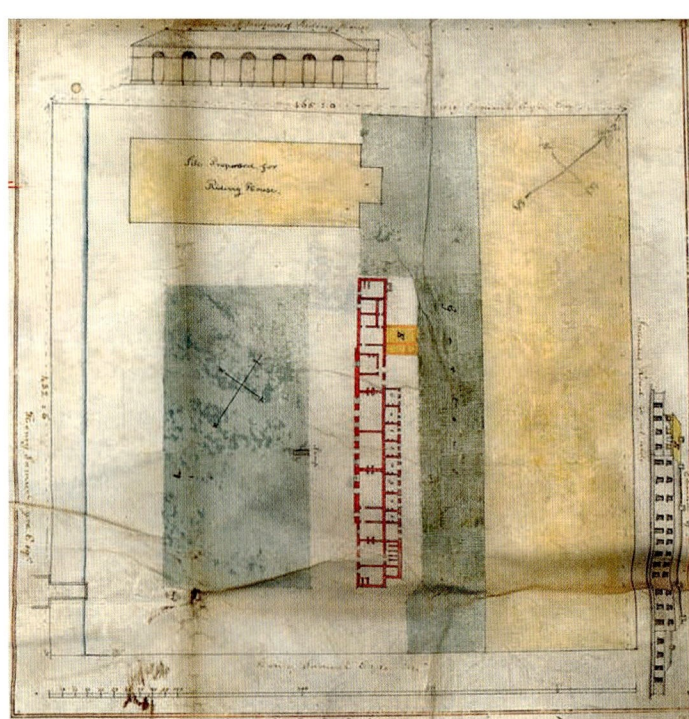

Plan view of proposed new Riding School, 1824.

These blocks, with a few obvious improvements over the years, such as the addition of washhouses and ablutions, stood from 1835 until they were demolished in 1970. Apart from the soldiery they also housed, for a short while, a few married families. This was in A Block at the eastern end of the building. In 2012, all that remained in the new barracks to remind us of these ancient buildings was the very high red brick wall behind the car park and senior non-commissioned officer's families quarters. The sojourn of the Recruits Depot at the Wood was even shorter than that of its predecessors—little more than a year. For the next two decades various detachments of Foot Guards and sometimes Infantry of the Line were in residence. Often these detachments comprised two or more companies of Guards or Line Infantry, sometimes less, sometimes more.

The sentry on the "Military Road"
(Light Dragoon)

Driver — 1815

Above: A sentry on the Military Road.

Right: A Driver from the Corps of Gunner Drivers practises a spot of community relations with the dairy maids!

Below: Hazards of the farm.

Occupational hazards – 1806–12

The Cavalry Riding Establishment at work, c.1830.

It was to be almost twenty years before the barracks echoed once again to the rattle of horses' hooves, when the Wood became home to the various regiments of the Household Cavalry—the impetus for the move being the rebuilding of the Household Cavalry Barracks in Hyde Park. Timber stables (which lasted until 1970) were erected, along with offices and an Officers' Mess. Their design, it is said, had been for use in the Crimea, and they were certainly similar to other such buildings used for the same purpose at Aldershot. Other changes to the barracks included the sub-division of the Riding School to create stores and tack rooms. On 25 October 1876 elements of the 1st Life Guards

Foot Guards drilling at the barracks, 1854.

took up residence. As the barracks at St. John's Wood were not big enough to accommodate the whole Regiment, it was split, with Regimental Headquarters at St. John's Wood and troops spread between the Wood, Kensington, Hampton Court and Regents Park Barracks. At this time the three Regiments of Household Cavalry, 1st and 2nd Life Guards and the Royal Horse Guards (The Blues) exchanged stations annually. Ceremonial duties were undertaken from Regents Park Barracks: the regiment at Knightsbridge being used for police work, after which they moved to the rural serenity of Combermere Barracks at Windsor. During the period 1876 to 1880 elements of all three regiments passed through St. John's Wood.

In the spring of 1880, Knightsbridge Barracks were ready for re-occupation and on 5th May the Royal Horse Guards moved in. Their place at Regents Park was taken by the 2nd Life Guards from Combermere, whilst the 1st Life Guards left the Wood for the last time and reassembled their scattered troops at Windsor. Six weeks later, on 24 June, A Battery A Brigade (later to become 'The Chestnut Troop') Royal Horse Artillery, commanded by Major S. J. Nicholson RHA, marched from Aldershot to take up residence at St. John's Wood. History does not relate as to whether it was intended to be a temporary occupation or if it was definitely planned to have an RHA battery permanently stationed in the capital. Whatever the motivation, it was undeniably a turning point in the history of both the Wood and the Royal Horse Artillery, marking the beginning of an era when the barracks had at last found a more permanent role than hitherto and with a regiment for whom the Wood became the home station of choice in the years to come.

Top: Combermere Barracks, Windsor *c.*1876.
Centre: Regents Park Barracks, *c.*1880.
Bottom: The new Hyde Park Barracks, 1880.

Chapter Two

ENTER
THE ROYAL HORSE ARTILLERY
1880–1906

The arrival of A Battery A Brigade at St. John's Wood Barracks in June 1880 does not appear to have been anything more than a matter of convenience for the War Office. Indeed, from the Distribution Lists of the period as well as battery records, it would seem that their stay at the barracks had more to do with their transit to Dublin from Aldershot than that of taking up duties in the capital. That said, their arrival set a precedent that has endured with few interruptions for more than 130 years, and their short stay would be the first of two occasions when the battery would be stationed at the 'Wood'.

No nation has carried its whole past so completely into the present.
With us historical associations are not matters of rhetorical reference
on great occasions; but they surround us in everything we do.
FROM MATHEW CREIGHTON, *THE ENGLISH NATIONAL CHARACTER*, 1896

Fitting a six-gun horse artillery battery of roughly 150 officers and men and up to 110 horses—not to mention 'followers' of women and children—into the much neglected barracks at St. John's Wood brought problems of its own as far as accommodation was concerned. There was no separate gun park—the guns being housed initially in a boarded-off area in the Riding School—and under the same roof there were soldiers' quarters, stores and a small hospital at the eastern end of the building (in later years part of this was known as the 'Staff Employed' accommodation). The saddler's shop and forge were in huts that extended south from the sick lines and pharmacy. By the middle of the 20th century these huts stopped short at the tailor's shop which then became adjacent to the Gun Park, believed to have been built shortly after the First World War.

A 'soldiers' hut' for 28 men jutted out into the square at the south-western corner, with an ablution house where the Morgan Lines were later to be—an area well known to soldiers of a later era. An infant and adult school and a recreation room stood more or less on the site of where the NAAFI and Dining Hall were later built (around 1921). The wooden horse lines which had been built to accommodate the Household Cavalry in 1870, are perpetuated in a splendid G. D. Giles painting, dated *c.*1888, a time when B Battery B Brigade, later L Battery RHA, were in residence, which has hung in the Cavalry Club since 1964. It is full of contemporary detail—hayracks on the wall and saddle racks at the end of each stall—the latter of which were still in use until 1969. Unfortunately, there is no title to the picture and no information on the back of the canvas which could throw any light on its earlier history. The

SWORD V. SWORD, MOUNTED

SPONGING OFF THE SCARS OF DISHONOUR

SLICING THE LEMONS

TILTING AT THE RING

TENT-PEGGING

ANNIHILATING THE TURKISH FORCES

Scenes from the activities on display at the Military Tournament and Assault at Arms held at the Agricultural Hall, Islington, in June 1880.

men and horses (dark bays) are depicted with great sympathy and obvious equestrian knowledge. The picture has become popular in recent years as the subject for a Christmas card.

The sojourn of A Battery A Brigade at St. John's Wood lasted only until 23 March 1881 when they departed for Dublin. Not much is recorded of their time at the Wood, certainly nothing of a ceremonial nature. They did, however, find time to carry out their annual 'Musketry' training at Pirbright during the autumn months of September and October, but

unfortunately little else of importance is mentioned until they departed in the early spring of the following year. It is possible that the battery embarked for Dublin at Woolwich, which would explain in some part the reason for their short stay at the Wood. They were replaced by G Battery C Brigade RHA, later 132 Battery (The Bengal Rocket Troop) RA. Fortunately this battery stayed a while longer, until May 1883, when they were replaced by C Battery, A Brigade RHA (now C Battery RHA) who arrived at the Wood from Ireland. C Battery remained at the

By 1884 the tournament included the driving competition for RHA and RA gun teams, seen here in the report of the time by the *Illustrated London News.*

barracks for three years, until April 1886, and during their stay they, too, were involved with the Military Tournament at Islington, although little else is recorded as far as ceremonial duties are concerned.

The arrival of B Battery B Brigade, (now L (Néry) Battery RHA) from Exeter, under command of Major E. S. B. Lockyer RHA marked a definite step-change in the fortunes of the barracks. It would appear that by now St. John's Wood had become accepted as a regular station for RHA batteries, although not one that included the exclusive role of State ceremonial. They were, however, gradually being drawn into the ceremonial duties of the capital and they were much in demand for public displays and exhibitions. The records for this battery contain several references to their successes at the 'Military Tournament at Islington' which began in 1880, and where 'No 2 Subdivision (a Sub-section in today's parlance) under Sgt. Thorpe won second prize in the Driving Competition'. They did rather better the following year when 'No 1 Subdivision under Sgt. Ward won first prize'.

These artillery driving competitions—in which gun teams preceded by the Number One negotiated a twisting course through gate-posts and pegs—generated a great deal of competition among both

RHA and RFA batteries at the time. The Royal Field Artillery with their heavier equipment competed against each other at the trot, Royal Horse Artillery at the gallop. The driving competitions continued to be staged until 1912, six years after the tournament had moved to Olympia, but were very much overshadowed by the musical drive, which from its first appearance, became one of the great attractions of the programme. As well as driving competitions there were also many Skill at Arms competitions which included 'Tilting at the Ring, Lemon Cutting and Tent-Pegging'. It was these competitions that were staged at the very first tournament: artillery driving and other displays being included a year or two later. The officers credited with the idea for a military tournament were Colonel Burnaby of the Royal Horse Guards and Colonel the Hon. A. Stewart, then Superintendent of the Riding Establishment RA, for 'the encouragement of Skill at Arms'. It is gratifying to know today that a member of the forebear of the King's Troop was partly responsible for the creation of what became the greatest military tournament in the world, and one at which the musical drive by the battery at the Wood became a firm favourite until its demise in 1999.

On 5 July 1887 B Battery B Brigade travelled from St. John's Wood to Aldershot where they took part

RHA Stables at St. John's Wood, a contemporary painting *c.*1888 by G. D. Giles.

in the great Jubilee Review before her 'Gracious Majesty The Queen Empress Victoria and most of the crowned heads of Europe' and 'the high state of efficiency of the battery was a matter of much comment'. It is further recorded that 'on 10 July at 5 p.m. the battery marched out of Aldershot for St. John's Wood, a distance of 41 miles, which they reached at 7 a.m. the following morning'.

A comment below this entry in the battery records states: 'a good performance considering they commenced the march in a severe thunderstorm'. [Having completed many a lengthy hack over similar distances with the King's Troop in later years, I very much agree with that comment and I have much empathy with those who took part in this journey!] On 1 May 1888 the battery departed St. John's Wood for Woolwich and took up its new quarters in the West Square. They were replaced by B Battery A Brigade from Aldershot. As with some of its predecessors, this battery spent little more than year at the barracks. On 1 July 1889 the brigade system was abolished and the battery was redesignated B Battery RHA and sailed for service in

India the following month. They were replaced by J Battery RHA from Abbassia, India. This battery stayed for just over two years, until 1891. Little is recorded of the period during which these two batteries were at the Wood, but it is safe to imagine that they too were much involved with the driving competitions at the Naval and Military Tournament as well as fulfilling their normal training requirements. For a short while the barracks lay unoccupied, but in 1893 D Battery RHA arrived from Meerut, India.

The period that this battery spent at the Wood has provided a rich seam of photographic material covering the cultural and military life of both the Wood and the battery. D Battery, of course, has, over the years, gained great fame and kudos from being the first battery to perform the now famous musical drive at the Naval and Military Tournament at the Agricultural Hall, Islington in 1895. An example of their fame is recorded in the Navy and Army Illustrated of 1896 where a photograph of the officers of the battery has the following comment below:

'D Battery RHA for the past three years has been

stationed at St. John's Wood, and the skill of its gunners in the musical ride (sic) at this year's Tournament will, doubtless be familiar to most of our readers'.

After three very eventful and successful years at the Wood, D Battery RHA exchanged places with G Battery at Woolwich en route to India and the transcript of service at the time records the event thus:

'On 26 October 1896 D Battery embarked at Southampton for Bombay on its third tour of Indian service. Strength: one Major, one Captain, three Lieutenants, one Battery Sergeant Major, one Staff Sergeant Farrier, 16 NCOs, two Trumpeters, four Artificers, 36 Gunners, 25 Drivers. Two Sergeants followed by a later ship'. On arrival at Umballa, the battery inherited 'one Battery Quartermaster Sergeant, 40 Gunners and 29 Drivers from N Battery RHA'. The battery had been armed with the 12-pounder BL gun of 6 cwt* (pole draught) and the writer laments the fact that they took over the 'antiquated 12-pdr BL gun of 7 cwt with shaft draught'.

The battery horses while in England are described as having been blacks with a 'great reputation for their splendid appearance'. Whilst those that they took over from N were bays and browns (Australian 'Walers', so called because they were bred in New South Wales) 'a fine lot of good quality and very active'.

It was during the period in which G Battery was at St. John's Wood that the first known photograph of a Royal Salute in St. James's Park was taken, in 1897. Apart from this and their annual appearances at the Royal Naval and Military Tournament there is little else recorded of their time in London. In the autumn of 1899 G Battery departed for service in the South African War. For a few months the barracks was without a tenant until the formation of V Battery RHA at Woolwich in February 1900. This battery arrived at the Wood in early 1901 and stayed for less than a year until it, too, was sent for service overseas, to Australia

An advertisement displaying the driving competition for the RHA gun teams. 'The Royal Military Tournament: the Victorian horse artillery in the driving competition—a sharp turn.'

as part of the Imperial Representative Corps.

At the turn of the 19th century St. John's Wood was still a very rural area, despite the rash of house building that had taken place during the previous thirty years. Although the farm and the animals had long gone it still had a very rustic air about it. The barracks were by now an established feature: the main entrance being located on what had become Ordnance Road; and by this time, quite conveniently, a Public House, complete with its own livery yard, had been established at the bottom of the road at the junction with Acacia Road.

On 10 February 1902, after a period of intermittent

D Battery gun team. First Prize at the Galloping Competition, Royal Naval and Military Tournament 1894. They are pictured outside the Officers' Mess at St. John's Wood Barracks. The trophy is being held by one of the two members of the detachment sitting on the limber. The present day Mess building stands roughly where this picture is taken.

The Bombardiers of D Battery pictured with a 12-pounder gun in the manège at the Wood in 1896. Immediately behind them are the officers' living quarters which became SNCO's (and the RSM's) married quarters in the 20th century. In 2012 this area was still part of the manège.

G Battery RHA fire a 41-gun salute in St. James's Park, 1897. This is the earliest known photograph of a battery in action for a Royal Salute.

use, the barracks became the home of X Battery RHA. It would appear from such records as are available that it was at this point in history that the battery at St. John's Wood became the officially nominated saluting battery for State occasions in the capital. Before they performed any State ceremonial however, they were first involved in the musical drive at the 'Military Tournament' in May 1902. It is recorded that the tournament was opened by His Majesty King Edward VII, and he 'expressed his approval of the performance of the battery to the Commanding Officer'. State ceremonial as we know it today was in its infancy at this time, but many of the procedures that continue to be used by the King's Troop have their origins here, at the beginning of the 20th century. Shortly after their performances at the military tournament, the battery proceeded to Okehampton by rail for Practice Camp. On return they prepared for the Coronation of King Edward VII. Their duties for this ceremony were described as follows:

'On 9 August 1902 paraded in Hyde Park and fired the Daybreak Salute at 4.36 a.m. (dawn would barely have broken at this time!) Paraded again in Hyde Park at 11.30 a.m., brigaded with Y RHA and the 16th Brigade-Division RFA, the whole under command of

Ordnance Road, St. John' Wood, 1900, looking north from the junction with Acacia Road. The barracks can be seen at the far right of the picture where the tree line begins. On the extreme left are the livery yard and the Ordnance Arms Public House, the latter of which still exists.

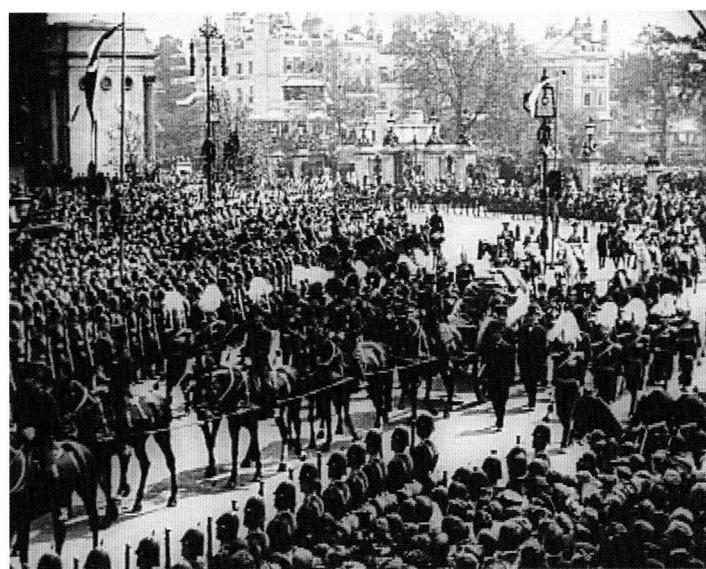

The funeral cortège of King Edward VII with the gun carriage of BB Battery RHA.

EAST END SIEGE. — After the battle: Firemen extinguishing the flames, and Scots Guards assembled.

'The barracks at St. John's Wood were much the same as they had always been. The stables and the officers' mess were wooden huts. The officers' quarters were in a building at the North East corner, later used as married quarters for senior NCOs. In the wooden mess-hut one room, divided in half by a curtain, served as dining room and ante-room; the kitchen and 'offices' were in another hut behind it. Breakfast and luncheon were provided but not dinner: except for the orderly officer when he had to be in during the evening, which was not often…'

As with many of their predecessors, the battery's principal duties in the annual calendar was to fire the salutes required for Royal birthdays and other State occasions. During their three years at the Wood, BB Battery's most important ceremonial duties included the funeral of King Edward VII in 1910 and the Coronation of King George V in 1911.

Between these two events, and far removed from any form of ceremonial, the battery played a minor role in one of the early 20th century's great dramas, when in January 1911 they were ordered to provide a section of guns to

The Sidney Street Siege 2 January 1911. **Top:** A report on the event at the time.

Bottom: A section of BB Battery RHA from St. John's Wood await orders after their arrival at Sidney Street.

assist in the infamous 'Sidney Street Siege'. In the event they were not required, and the siege ended with a battle between the anarchists, the police and troops from the nearby Guards battalion.

For the funeral of King Edward VII the battery was detailed to provide a team of eight black horses to draw the 18-pounder gun carriage that would carry the coffin of the King. The gun carriage was provided by the Royal Arsenal. The coffin was transported from Buckingham Palace on 17 May 1910 to Westminster Hall, to lie in State, and on the 20th to carry it from thence to Paddington Station for the journey to Windsor. Opinion varies as to why the battery was warned to use an eight horse team for the 18-pounder as opposed to the six horse team ordinarily used for both the 13-pounder and 18-pounder guns It is likely however, that they were merely copying the precedent set at Queen Victoria's funeral when her coffin, borne upon a field gun, was drawn by eight horses of the Royal Hanoverian Creams and driven by the Royal Postilions. Whatever the reason, it was never repeated at subsequent State funerals.

Originally BB was to have transported King Edward's coffin at Windsor, but the Navy asserted the claim they had established by stepping into the breach nine years before, and the privilege was accorded to them. However, the Battery had

plenty to do without the Windsor duty. Their first task was a Salute of Minute Guns, fired from what was then the usual position on the grass just inside the railings of St. James's Park, at the east end of the lake. It took place on 7 May 1910, after which there was an interval of ten days before the King's funeral. Rehearsals for the funeral ceremonies took place at the crack of dawn each morning to try and avoid publicity, something that would have been a little easier then than now. Every precaution was taken to prevent the horses from shying. There were visits to Chelsea Barracks where they drove past ranks of guardsmen practising rifle drill, to the Riding School at Regents Park Barracks, where the Household Cavalry Band received them with blasts of the appropriate music, and finally to Paddington Station where the Station Master managed to make all the engine drivers blast their engine whistles.

The rigorous preparations were well worthwhile, and on the day all the Battery's various duties were successfully accomplished. Almost every man and horse must have been on parade for this occasion, with the Commanding Officer leading the black team drawing the gun carriage, attended by full detachments of mounted NCOs and gunners, while the remainder of the battery fired a Royal Salute in Hyde Park.

The funeral team of BB Battery RHA for King Edward VII, on the square in front of the soldiers barrack block at St. John's Wood Barracks, 1910. Most of these horses went on to serve in France with F Battery during the First World War.

The Drivers of F Battery RHA Musical Drive, at the Royal Naval and Military Tournament, Olympia, 1914.

The famous painting by Fortunio Matania of L Battery RHA at Néry, 1 September 1914. Virtually annihilated during this epic battle, the battery was reformed at St. John's Wood in November 1914.

The Coronation of King George V followed during the next year and, compared with the funeral, provided very few problems. On the day of the service the battery fired two salutes from the north bank of the Serpentine, the first at sunrise and the second to coincide with the placing by the Archbishop of the Coronation Crown on the head of the King. For the second salute there was a small crowd of spectators and while the battery was at a position of 'stand easy', away from the gun line, 'friends and relations were able to come and talk to the detachments'. In those days, the saluting battery was always provided with an escort from the Household Cavalry to and from the saluting base. On this occasion the escort was provided by the Royal Horse Guards (The Blues). The long procession through London took place the day after the Coronation Service and lasted four hours. For this the battery turned out two sections, each of two guns and two ammunition wagons with full detachments of 17 men with drawn swords in each section. One section was in front and the other at the rear of the Royal Carriage.

The annual calendar of events for the battery at the Wood followed a now familiar pattern: In late

J Battery RHA in action on the Western Front 1916. Many of these horses came from F Battery at St. John's Wood on the outbreak of war in 1914.

spring and early summer of each year preparations for the musical drive had been one of the dominant themes of activity at the Wood since the drive's first inclusion in the programme of the 'Royal Military and Naval Tournament' in 1895.

In those days, batteries changed station roughly every two or three years. Thus, preparing for the musical drive during the first year of residence was an anxious business, especially as everyone knew that their experienced predecessors would be passing critical comments from the sidelines. As ever, many of BB's horses had been on strength for many years and the career of one veteran 'Bruiser' No. 65 is worthy of note. A small compact horse who spent most of his time as a 'wheeler', he had been with the battery for ten years. When BB left the Wood in 1911 he was taken over by F Battery RHA and went to Belgium with them in October 1914. He survived the war and after he came home was given Royal hospitality by Queen Alexandra and ended his days at Sandringham.

The arrival of F Battery by train from Ipswich on 20 October 1911 marked the first of three tours of duty in the capital for this battery over the next 30 years. On arrival they took over the horses (all blacks) and all the harness and equipment except for the guns from BB. They then became on the 'Higher Establishment of 170 Rank and File, 135 horses (including officers), six guns and six wagons'. Their first ceremonial duty took place on 1 December 1911 when they fired a 41-gun salute in St. James's Park for the anniversary of HM Queen Alexandra's birthday.

The following year began with miscellaneous ceremonial duties including the provision of a gun carriage for several military funerals, including that of the Japanese Military attaché, in January, and the Duke of Fife, at Windsor in late February. In those days duties outside London usually resulted in a day's march before and after the event. Ceremonial duties were put aside in April when the battery marched to Salisbury Plain for 'annual gun practice'. On return to the Wood in early May they resumed training for the musical drive at the Royal Naval and Military Tournament, which took place at Olympia from 22 May until 7 June 1912.

This was F Battery's first year at the Royal Tournament, and there was, as might be expected, much apprehension as to how the battery would compare with the performances of its predecessor. In the event, all went extremely well and the drivers of F were complimented on the 'excellence of the drives' by HRH the Duke of Connaught. The calendar of events for the remainder of the year included the usual gun salutes and State ceremonial as well as route-lining duties. In June the battery provided '89 NCOs and men to line the route from Victoria for the visit of the French President'. Life at St. John's Wood continued in a manner not too unfamiliar to later generations. In March 1913 for example, the battery provided two gun teams for the Easter 'Van Horse Parade' in Regents Park, an event under a slightly different title that continues to this day, and received many compliments on the turnout of the horses and the bearing of the men on parade. Later that year the battery had the honour of providing a gun carriage for the funeral of Field Marshal Viscount Wolseley, one of Britain's famous 19th-century commanders.

The year 1914 began for F in similar vein. The usual gun salutes were fired and there were several State visits. In early May they turned out 60 NCOs and men for route-lining duties for the State visit of the King of Denmark. Shortly afterwards, on 14th of the month, they moved to Olympia to perform the musical drive at the Royal Naval and Military Tournament. Once again they received many plaudits for the quality of the drive in particular, warm compliments were paid by HM King George V. Sadly, war clouds were looming in Europe and this would be the last tournament for F for some considerable time. On 5 June the battery marched to Salisbury Plain for annual gun practice, for which they received a good report. They returned to the Wood on 11 July.

At 6.25 a.m. on the morning of 4 August 1914 mobilisation was ordered and as F were an unallocated battery, they were commanded to send to J Battery RHA at Aldershot, (with whom they were loosely brigaded) two officers, two SNCOs, 102 NCOs and men and 112 horses. On 9 September the battery left St. John's Wood for camp prior to embarkation for France. The barracks lay empty once more.

In the autumn of 1914 L Battery, which had been all but destroyed in the heroic action with 1st Cavalry Brigade at Néry on 1 September, was reformed at St. John's Wood with four 18-pounder guns. They were brigaded with B and Y batteries as XV Brigade RHA and joined the famous 29th Division. They embarked at Avonmouth for Gallipoli in March 1915. Later that year a reserve training brigade was formed at St. John's Wood barracks with the purpose of training young officers in equitation. Many of the officers and permanent staff for this establishment came from the former Riding Establishment at Woolwich, which had virtually ceased to exist on the outbreak of war. Among the officers was a newly commissioned Lieutenant and Riding Master named J. E. Hance, who had been a sergeant major instructor at Woolwich before the war. He gave a very detailed account of life at the Wood during this period in his book *Riding Master*. The barracks, of course, changed not at all during the war years, but other parts of St. John's Wood, such as Lord's Cricket Ground, were requisitioned to provide more space for outdoor manèges and accommodation for the hundreds of officers who passed through the brigade during the war years. The training brigade was finally disbanded at the end of 1918.

Lt. & Riding Master J. E. Hance of the RHA training brigade demonstrating jumping techniques, with his horse Harlequin, over the guns and a wire fence in the manège at St. John's Wood Barracks, 1917.

The gun team of black horses of F Battery RHA on return from Germany in 1919. These were all that survived from the 112 horses loaned to J Battery at the beginning of the war. The lead driver, G. Tofts, took over his pair in 1911 and was with them continuously for eight years, while the wheel driver H. R. Barnes, looked after his pair throughout the war. All of these horses were retired to Windsor Great Park after taking part in the ceremony of dedication for the Unknown Warrior in 1920.

On 4 May 1919 F Battery returned to St. John's Wood from Germany having formed part of the Army of Occupation. The battery strength was one officer and 50 Other Ranks, including 14 NCOs and men who had marched out from the Wood for France in 1914. In June the battery was ordered to form part of the 3rd Brigade RHA along with D Battery from Colchester and J Battery from Canterbury and to embark for service in India in early 1920. During the summer months of 1919, while the Army was reorganised to peacetime requirements, the battery received more than 100 men to bring it up to strength, as well as four 18-pounders and about 40 horses, including seven of the 112 black horses lent to J Battery for the period of the war in August 1914. This team of black horses were all now old, having been on parade with BB Battery at the funeral of King Edward in 1910. They were finally given an honoured and comfortable old age grazing in Windsor Park. On 27 January 1920 F Battery departed from St. John's Wood and embarked at Tilbury Docks on SS *Prinz Ludwig* for India. They were replaced at the Wood by N Battery RHA from Trowbridge.

Among the first duties carried out by N at the Wood was to provide a gun carriage and team of black horses for the ceremony of interment of the Unknown

Warrior at Westminster Abbey on Armistice Day, 11 November 1920. Coincidentally, some of the black horses used in the gun carriage for this solemn occasion had been with F and J Batteries both during and prior to the First World War; one or two had even been with BB Battery for the funeral of King Edward VII in 1910. By any standards they were 'old hands' as far as State ceremonial was concerned.

In late 1920 a programme of modernisation began at the barracks which included the demolition of the old wooden Officers Mess, the barrack hut at the south western corner of the square and the school building at the east end of the barracks. In their place came a new neoclassical-style officers' mess, and a similar style of building that housed the soldiers' cookhouse and the Navy Army and Air Force Institute canteen, known to soldiers of every generation as the 'NAAFI'. At the western end of the barracks, the barrack building that had jutted out onto the square was demolished, as was part of the wooden buildings that housed various offices and sick lines. A new Gun Park was built on this site. The programme of works was completed by the middle of the following year and the layout of the barracks now remained almost unaltered for the next 50 years, until the demolition and rebuilding programme for the new barracks began in 1970.

Clockwise from top:
The arrival of the Unknown Warrior at Victoria Railway Station—November 1920 and the gun team from N Battery RHA.

Passing along Whitehall.

The gun carriage passing the Cenotaph, November 11 1920.

The gun carriage of N Battery RHA passing through Wellington Arch, November 11 1920. This gun team included a few of the horses that had served throughout the First World War with F Battery RHA.

Chapter Four

THE END OF AN ERA
1921–1939

This period of just 18 years was marked by many national and historic occasions in which the saluting battery at the Wood played a prominent part. N Battery was in residence from early 1920 and they had the honour of carrying the Unknown Warrior to his last resting place at Westminster Abbey in November of that year. They also had the distinction of performing the musical drive at the first Royal Tournament after the War in May 1921. Change however, was in the air. The experience of the First World War and the introduction of motor transport had shown that the place of the horse in War was now limited. On the outbreak of the Second World War in September 1939, the last RHA battery at the Wood, and the last horsed RHA battery in existence, K Battery, was mechanized. For the duration of the War, St. John's Wood Barracks became the home of London District Signal Troop.

> ELLEN: *Things aren't what they used to be you know—it's all changing.*
> JANE: *Yes, I see it is.*
> NOEL COWARD, CAVALCADE, 1932

Life for N Battery soon developed into the customary routine of State ceremonial. The battery records their first year at the Wood as follows 'Since its arrival in London the Troop has fired all the ceremonial salutes, and has provided the gun carriage for many military funerals, including the Burial of the Unknown Warrior. The Musical Drive at the Royal Tournament has been done by "the Eagle Troop" this year (1921). Few people fully realise the months of practice and hard work that are necessary before the actual performances. Apart from knowledge of the figures, every driver must know his job thoroughly. Horses must be trained and very fit if they are to stand the strain of two performances a day for more than a fortnight. The musical drive is performed before very critical audiences, and the Battery, representing as it does, the Royal Horse Artillery, must show itself "worthy of its former fame"'.

Although the Royal Tournament no longer exists, I am sure similar sentiments can be echoed today by those serving with the King's Troop.

Early in 1922, much of N Battery left St. John's Wood for Ireland to form part of a Royal Artillery Mounted Rifle Regiment and to assist with the security arrangements during the transitional period when the country was divided between the new Irish Free State in the south and the British province of Ulster in the North. A small battery Cadre was left at the barracks during this period. However, before they departed in the spring of that year, they had time to celebrate Hyderabad Day. Battery records relate events at the time thus: 'The anniversary of the Battle of Hyderabad (1843) was celebrated by N Battery RHA (The Eagle Troop) on 24 March at St. John's Wood Barracks. The whole

N Battery RHA perform the 'Star' at the finale of the Musical Drive at the Royal Tournament at Olympia in 1921.

day was devoted to sports, in which all were very keen to participate, and although on account of the ground it was not practicable to hold a large number of mounted events, jumping was held in the riding school and musical chairs, mounted tug-of-war, etc. in the manège. In the evening a dinner was given in the new Regimental Institute (The NAAFI and Dining Hall to later generations), for past and present members of the "Eagle Troop" which 212 attended with Major G. M. Spencer-Smith DSO, Commanding, in the Chair. The entertainment in the evening was concluded with a 'Smoker' (an event at which amateur entertainments were carried out by those present—a tradition that appears to have all but died out in the Regiment today). On the following Monday the 'Eagle Troop' Ball was held in the Drill Hall of a local Armoured Car Company which was kindly loaned for the occasion'.

During this period, N were in Ireland—their duties in London and at the Royal Tournament being carried out largely by O Battery RHA, who, as part of 5th Brigade RHA, were stationed at Aldershot. A few months after their return from duty in Ireland, in October 1923, N Battery exchanged places with O Battery and joined 5th Brigade RHA. O Battery was by now quite conversant with the duties required of them at St. John's Wood and had become most proficient in performing the musical drive at the Royal Tournament. The most important duty for the battery during their time at the Wood took place on 18 October 1925 when they provided the gun team and detachment for the dedication ceremony at the unveiling of the new Royal Artillery War memorial at Hyde Park Corner.

The preparations and arrangements for this ceremony were quite exact. The wreath was made of laurels (the poppy had yet to be adopted), with sprigs of tightly banded red roses and sprigs of rosemary inserted 'for remembrance'. To protect it from the weather the card was framed and glazed. The frame itself was made from the wood of broken crosses found on the graves of artillerymen whose bodies had been removed from the Somme battlefield. The gun on which the wreath was carried was the No. 4 Gun of E Battery, which had fired the first artillery

O Battery RHA at the Royal Tournament in 1922. Jones is in the hand lead of the second team from the left and Othello in hand lead of the first team from the left.

shell of the Great War. The horses for the gun team, found by O Battery, included two leaders, Jones and Othello (formerly Joubert) that had gone to France with J Battery on the out-break of war in 1914 and went through the whole war, including the march to the Rhine. On the brow-bands of their head collars were stitched the ribbons of the three medals awarded for such service: the 1914 star, the British War Medal and the Victory Medal. This was their last parade before retirement. The gun of L Battery RHA from the battle at Néry and usually housed in the Imperial War Museum, was placed 'in action' on the island on which the Memorial stands.

Shortly after this duty, O Battery were once again at the forefront of a State occasion when they provided the gun team for the funeral of Queen Alexandra, the dowager widow of the late King Edward VII, on 27 November 1925. So pleased was the King with the arrangements for the funeral and the conduct of O Battery, that he instructed the Lord Chamberlain to publish the following special district order:

'I have received the King's command to instruct you to convey to all ranks under your command during yesterday's ceremony for the funeral of her late Majesty Queen Alexandra an expression of his Majesty's thanks for their services on this solemn occasion. The King is fully conscious of the severe and trying conditions under which these duties were performed by all ranks, more especially by the Royal Horse Artillery, whose responsibilities were increased by reason of the unfavourable weather conditions'. Lord Ruthven stated that he had much pleasure in publishing the letter and he added 'In doing so I wish to congratulate Lt. Col. A. K. Main DSO and all ranks O Battery RHA on the admirable manner in which their extremely difficult and responsible duty was carried out'. By the end of the following year O Battery had exchanged places with M Battery and departed for Aldershot and 1st Brigade RHA.

During the following three years M Battery also received many plaudits for their standard of bearing and turnout on ceremonial parades as well as for the quality of the musical drive at the Royal Tournament. Gilbert Holiday produced two splendid pastel paintings of M Battery at Olympia and they have, in many ways, immortalised the precision and panache of a display that has come to epitomise the very soul and spirit of the Royal Horse Artillery at its best. M Battery departed from St. John's Wood for Aldershot and 3rd Brigade RHA in October 1929 and was replaced by J Battery from the same. The battery strength of J RHA at the Wood in January 1930 is recorded as being 'Six officers, 116 Other Ranks, 72 Light Draught horses and ten chargers.' Not too much of a difference from the strength of the newly formed Riding Troop RHA of 1946, or indeed, the King's Troop of today.

As was the custom and procedure at the time, many of the horses and men were taken over from M Battery. The first important event for the battery in 1930 was the inspection of their horses by the Assistant Director of Remounts, Brigadier C. L. Rowe, in February. His report was very complimentary stating 'Condition of animals—very good. Average age on 1 November 1929 11 years 7 months. A well horsed unit, a few need to be changed. The turnout was excellent.' Shortly afterwards the battery provided a gun team for the Hunter and Light Draught Horse show at Islington. This became almost an annual event in the calendar of the battery at the Wood, not too much different from the annual Easter Parade in Regents Park, in which the King's Troop takes part. Apart from the usual military duties of salutes and funeral guns, March is also the month when training for the musical drive begins a tradition that continues to this day. At this time the battery

A pastel painting by Gilbert Holiday of the musical drive of O Battery RHA at the Royal Tournament 1924.

at the Wood often used the arena at Albany Street Barracks, Regents Park, to practise the drive at the trot, before progressing to the canter and the training ground at Wormwood Scrubs. Another traditional event during spring is the annual administrative inspection by the GOC London District. For J Battery this took place on 30 April and, as for today, the battery was mounted in full ceremonial dress.

Recruiting in the 1930s was as challenging then as ever it has been and the comments in the battery history record this: 'Owing to the ease with which all people can get the Dole, recruiting has fallen off, even for the Gunners (which must have been a popular choice at the time) so we get ten overseas details posted to us from AA, Heavy and Field units to make up our numbers.' Despite this the standard of turnout, horses, and guns continued to be maintained to that expected of the RHA. On 25 May the Royal Tournament party left the Wood for Olympia; strength: one officer, 65 NCOs and men, 48 horses, six 13-pounders and

The watercolour painting by Gilbert Holiday of 'M' Battery performing the Musical Drive at Olympia in 1928.

J Battery gun teams practise the musical drive at Albany Street Barracks, March 1930.

one spare limber. The opening performance took place on the 29 May in front of HM Queen Mary, The King being too unwell to attend. On 3 June the battery fired the annual 41-gun salute in Hyde Park in honour of King George V's birthday. The firing of salutes and other ceremonial events during the Royal Tournament was quite common in the days before the date was changed to July (in the late 1960s). On 27 July the battery departed by train from Paddington Station for annual firing camp at Trawsfynydd; strength: six officers, 61 Light Draught horses, ten chargers, 89 OR—no guns. At this time J Battery's operational role was as a 4.5-inch battery in support of 1st Brigade RHA. Thus they would draw up their guns on arrival from the camp pool. This, it was stated 'was in the interests of the new economy, which is very marked in Army estimates' (not unlike the deficit of today!).

The horse lines at Trawsfynydd camp, a sketch by Gilbert Holiday. This sketch is a reminder of the (often) spells of misery, mud and moisture endured by both stable guards and their long faced friends whilst at camp.

TRAWSFYNYDD 1928

The War Office is taking part in the Hunters' Improvement and National Light Horse Breeding Society's Show to be held at the Agricultural Hall, on March, 4-5-6.

Photograph shows, Brigadier-General Rome, inspecting the Gun team, which is to be exhibited at the Show. *Photopress*.

Gun teams of J Battery at St. John's Wood Barracks in 1930. This scene will be recognised by several generations of Horse Gunners who have served at the Wood. Indeed the barracks changed little from the time when these photographs were taken in 1930 to their demolition in 1970.

Photograph shows, War Office Officials inspecting the Gun Team what is to be exhibited at the Show. *Photopress*.

Of the many interesting duties that the battery performed during their time at the Wood, one of the most unusual and famous were the arrangements for the funeral of those killed in the R101 airship disaster in June 1930. For this occasion J Battery were required to temporarily house 80 horses, 77 men and two officers from Woolwich in the riding school and various other parts of the barracks. Given that there were married quarters also in the barracks at the

THE ROYAL TOURNAMENT.
OPENING AT OLYMPIA ON MAY 23RD.

The Musical Ride will be by the 17th/21st Lancers and " M " Bty. R.H.A., whose musical drive has been a feature of the recent Tournaments, will give a farewell display, as the Battery leaves London for duty at Aldershot at the end of the year.

R.H.A. DRIVERS IN PRE-WAR UNIFORM.

A sketch by Gilbert Holiday for the 'Gunner' magazine advertising M Battery's role in the Royal Tournament, 1929.

time (Jubilee Buildings had yet to be built) the Wood must have been bursting at the seams!

J Battery's performances of the musical drive at the Royal Tournament in the early 1930s were, as ever, extremely well received. Indeed, the following report appeared in Gunner magazine:

'Why do the trumpeters of J Battery, who gave the musical drive with great dash and finish carry silver trumpets with crimson silk guidons, on which are embroidered "Java Nagpore" above and Mahidpore below a crown and laurel wreath? The distinction dates from 1817 when the battery, then known as the "Flying Artillery" of the Madras Horse Artillery, was mainly responsible for the victory over the army of Mulhar Ras Holkhar'.

J Battery served at the Wood until September 1932, when they exchanged places with F (Sphinx) Battery of 3rd Brigade RHA at Aldershot. As the batteries at the Wood were on the lower establishment of four guns only, the Left Section of F Battery comprising; three sergeants, three bombardiers, 37 gunners, nine drivers, two trumpeters and 33 horses, remained at Aldershot with J Battery. This was the third and last tour of duty for F at the Wood.

The first ceremonial duty for the battery in 1932 was the Minute Guns (then known as 'Signal Guns')

Above and opposite page: A brochure for the Royal Tournament of 1932 featuring the musical drive of J Battery RHA from St. John's Wood.

at Horse Guards Parade on Armistice Day. Thereafter the routine was as familiar to later generations at the Wood as it was to those at the time. In April 1932 the battery provided two gun carriages for the funeral of General Sir Webb Gillman, GOC Eastern Command. Unusually, the gun salute of 17 Minute Guns was fired from Chelsea Gardens rather than St. James's or Hyde Park. On 21 May the battery proceeded to Olympia to perform the musical drive at the Royal Tournament. As was now customary, they received many plaudits for the quality of the drive and the standard of bearing and turnout of the drivers and horses. The last year of the battery's service at the Wood, from the summer of 1935 until their departure in the autumn of 1936, included some of the most historic events in British social history. The first took place on 6 May 1935 when F Battery together with D Battery of 3rd Brigade RHA, formed part of the cavalry representatives for the procession of their Majesties the King and Queen to St. Paul's Cathedral on the occasion of their Silver Jubilee.

One other significant change took place at the Wood during 1935 with the construction of 68 soldiers' married quarters on the west side of the camp. This required the demolition of a row of terraced houses in Queen's Terrace, the remainder of which still stand at the northern end, beginning with the Knights

Bubbles. A great favourite with both N and J Batteries with whom she served since 1920, she is pictured here in front of the Regimental Institute and Dining Hall at St. John's Wood Barracks with the Officers' Cart shortly before she was destroyed in the summer of 1932 aged 19 years.

The funeral gun team of J Battery pictured on the square in 1932. The old terraced houses at the back of the barracks were replaced in 1935 by the 'new' Jubilee Buildings' for use by married soldiers.

MUSICAL DRIVE

by

" J " BATTERY ROYAL HORSE ARTILLERY

THE Drive is carried out by six 13-pounder guns drawn by six six-horse teams.
    After forming up in the arena, the teams march past in line and salute, while the Band plays the " Royal Artillery Slow March." They then go straight off at a gallop in pairs from the centre and wheel outwards. After performing various simple turns, inclines and circles, one half battery changes rein, and the movement known as the " Scissors " is carried out. The two half batteries then form up at the ends of the arena, the " Charge " is sounded, and the teams gallop through each other, wheel round the ends of the arena by half batteries and then wheel into line at close interval.

They then trot out of the arena in Battery Column.

HISTORY

The Battery was raised in 1756 as Madras Horse Artillery.

The present designation dates from 1889.

It served in the Mysore, Mahratta and Java Wars, and in the Indian Mutiny.

It went through the whole of the South African War, 1899-1902, and was sent to France in August, 1914, and served throughout the War in France and Belgium with the 2nd Cavalry Division.

A gun team of black horses from F Battery carries the body of King George V from Sandringham to Wolferton Station.

A pastel painting by Gilbert Holiday of F Battery passing through Marble Arch on their way to fire a Royal Salute in Hyde Park, 1936.

A gun team of F Battery at the funeral of the German Ambassador, Carlton Terrace, London, 1936.

The funeral procession proceeds along the King's Road.

The battery formed up on the square at St. John's Wood barracks ready for the march to Woolwich.

The battery prepares the 'King's Gun' which carried King George V prior to its presentation to the Royal Artillery Depot, Woolwich.

F Battery depart from St. John's Wood Barracks for Woolwich with the 'King's Gun'.

'They're off', a sketch by Gilbert Holiday of the battery gun teams about to enter the arena for the musical drive at Olympia, 1936.

of St. John Public House. Not surprisingly perhaps the new block was named 'Jubilee Buildings'. The fixtures and fittings for these flats changed hardly at all over the years and many still had panelled doors and brass fitments as well as open fires until their refurbishment in the mid-1970s.

As part of the gradual mechanisation of the Army and the removal of horse-powered traction in October 1935, F Battery received five gun teams from 3rd Brigade RHA. They included one big bay team from D Battery, a marvellous big brown team and a smaller bay team from J Battery. They were now 'as well horsed as they had ever been'.

The second most important event for the battery occurred on 20 January 1936 when King George V died. The following day the battery fired a 41-gun salute from Hyde Park to mark the proclamation of the accession of King Edward VIII. Later that day a funeral party with a 13-pounder gun was despatched to Sandringham to convey the body of the King to Wolferton Station. On arrival at King's Cross the train was met by a gun team with the 18-pounder gun that had been used at King Edward VII's funeral in 1910, commanded by Lt. Col. Duncan, the Battery Commander. The whole cortege then proceeded to Westminster Hall for the Lying-in-State. On 28 January the battery provided the 13-pounder gun (the Sandringham gun) on which the Royal Navy drew the coffin of the late King. During the funeral procession the battery fired the Minute Guns from Hyde Park. On 22 March 1936 the battery, mounted in full ceremonial order, attended at Woolwich for the handing over of the funeral gun, 'The King's Gun', to the Royal Artillery Depot.

F Battery horse lines at Olympia 1936. This splendid scene will be as familiar to those who served with the King's Troop in the 1950s and 60s and visitors to the Royal Tournament at Earls Court, as it was to the pre-war gunners and visitors of the time.

Apart from the usual excitement of the Royal Tournament during the summer, the remainder of their last year at the Wood passed without incident or special event. In early September they handed over the guns and horses, and some of the men, to K Battery RHA from Newport and sailed from Southampton on the 25 September for India and service at Risalpur in the North West Frontier Province.

Little did the officers and men of K realise in the autumn of 1936 as they settled into their new home in this leafy and quite tranquil area of north London and prepared for the Armistice Day

F Battery rehearsing the musical drive at Wormwood Scrubs training ground, 1936.

Top: K Battery coming into action at Hyde Park to fire a royal salute to mark the first anniversary of the coronation of King George VI and Queen Elizabeth, 12 May 1938.

Centre: The gun detachment unload the cartridge cases from the limber and prepare them for firing.

Bottom: The first round is fired at the appointed time.

ceremony, that they would be the last active horsed battery to serve at the Wood.

The most important event for the battery during their first year of ceremonial duties took place on 12 May 1937 with the coronation of the new King and Queen. For this event K Battery were part of the procession with four guns and full detachments. The Royal Salute that day was fired by J Battery of 3rd Brigade RHA. Thereafter life at the Wood followed the normal routine of training for both salutes and the musical drive. Many of the horses and men had been at the Wood for some years, remaining with each battery that arrived. Some of the horses bore names from the batteries in which they first served, such as Jasper from J and Foxy from F. It was a happy unit with most men enjoying a true love of horses. For some however, there was a hint of sadness at the prospect of mechanization.

LEAD DRIVERS

Top: K Battery rehearse the musical drive and the annual administrative parade at Wormwood Scrubs training ground, 1938.

Centre: The Battery Commander de-briefs the drivers at the end of the rehearsal.

Bottom: The battery rehearse the march past for the General Officer Commanding London District.

A gun team from K Battery passes Buckingham Palace with the coffin of Queen Maud of Norway, the last child of King Edward VII, en route for Victoria Railway Station, in 1938.

With war clouds looming over Europe in the summer of 1938, K continued with the normal routine of duties in the capital and practice camp at Larkhill, but change was in the air. On the outbreak of war in September 1939 the battery was mobilised at St. John's Wood, initially as a horsed battery. All non-essential stores and equipment, including much of the battery property and including some silver, were placed in the now vacant mobilisation store (which received a direct hit during the blitz on London in 1940). Shortly afterwards the horses were returned to the remount depot and K moved to Gloucestershire as a mechanized battery to form the nucleus of the new 5th Regiment RHA. Thereafter the barracks became the home of London District Signal Troop until the formation of the Riding Troop in early 1946.

K Battery RHA mobilised for war as a horsed gun battery at St. John's Wood Barracks, September 1939.

Jones and Othello

This pair of chestnut-coloured lead horses has become something of a legend in the history of the Royal Horse Artillery. They joined J Battery at Aldershot in 1914. Othello was then named Joubert and they served throughout the war, taking part in most of the main battles and actions. In 1919 after the Armistice they, among others, were posted to O Battery. It was at this point that Joubert was renamed Othello. When the battery returned to Aldershot later that year the Battery Commander at the time, Major A. K. Main DSO, knowing that they were going into stables which J Battery had occupied before the war told their drivers to let them loose to see where they went. They made straight for their pre-war stables and stalls!

While at Aldershot, Brigadier Willie Clark, then commanding 1st Brigade RHA, chose Jones as his model for a silver statuette of a typical RHA gun leader, which he presented to the RA Mess at Aldershot. The statuette is now the property of the King's Troop RHA.

The historic photograph of Jones and Othello at the dedication ceremony for the RA War Memorial on 18 October 1925. The ribbons of the war medals to which they were entitled are clearly visible on their brow bands.

"O" Battery
The Royal Horse Artillery
(The Rocket Troop)

Name...JONES... Position...LEAD OF GUN...

Age...19... Joined "O" Battery R.H.A...1-4-19...
ALDERSHOT COMMAND HORSE SHOW.
1920. 1ST PRIZE REGIMENTAL COACH.
1920. 2ND " GUN TEAM.
1921. 1ST " COACH TEAM.
1921. 1ST " LIGHT DRAUGHT TEAM.
1921. 1ST " COACHING MARATHON.
1922. 1ST " REGIMENTAL COACH.
1922. 2ND " GUN TEAM.
1922. 1ST " LIGHT DRAUGHT TEAM.
1923. 1ST " COACHING MARATHON.
1923. 2ND " { RICHMOND ROYAL HORSE SHOW.
           COACHING MARATHON.
1923. 2ND " GUN TEAM. ALDERSHOT.
1923. 2ND " REGIMENTAL COACH. ALDERSHOT.
SERVED THROUGHOUT THE GREAT WAR
           1914 - 1918 FRANCE.

Gale & Polden, Ltd. Aldershot.   9984-c

Jones's record of shows and service with O Battery RHA and the silver statuette of Jones commissioned by Brigadier Willie Clark.

Jones and Othello were typical of the light draught horse used by the horse and field artillery batteries at the time and indeed until mechanisation in 1939. They were the active 'vanner' of civilian life, the work horse of the Hackney Cab and sundry other commercial organisations. Height, 15.3 hands at 4 years, and though no one pretended they were blood stock and were commonly known as 'hairies', they did sterling work for the Regiment and well repaid the care and affection that were bestowed upon them.

Major Probert leads Jones, with Othello and a farm worker, into the fields at Bures, Suffolk.

This marvellous pair of horses continued to serve together in O Battery until 1925, during which time they won many prizes whilst working in the wheel of coach teams at coaching marathons, as well as several gun team classes in the lead. They also took part in countless performances of the musical drive at the Royal Tournament. Fortunately the story of these two horses has a happy ending. On retirement they were purchased by an officer serving with O Battery at the time, Major Ynyr Probert MC, and they spent their final years at the family farm in Bures, Suffolk.

Jones and Othello on the farm at Bures, Suffolk in 1926 with Major Probert's niece Margaret. They are standing in exactly the same position as when they were in the gun teams!

The Coaching Competition at Aldershot in which they won First Prize. Jones is the nearside wheel horse.

Chapter Five

THE KING'S TROOP
1945—1971

In early 1945 the barracks were still occupied by London District Signal Troop, but as a result of the end of hostilities in Europe there were moves afoot for change. Later that year HM The King expressed the wish that a horse-drawn battery might be stationed again in London for ceremonial duties, which, he further hoped, might be performed in the customary manner. Thus, early in 1946 the War Office issued instructions that the Riding Troop RHA should be formed on 17 April. This was to be the embodiment of the old Riding House Troop that had been disbanded at Woolwich on the outbreak of war in 1939. As there was no suitable accommodation or training ground immediately available in London the Troop was formed at Shoeburyness. They moved to the old battery station of St. John's Wood on 15 May 1946 and on receipt of their guns (18-pounder Mk II) began a month of intensive training for the King's Birthday Salute on 13 June.

'I am not getting any new flags though, only using an old one I had left over from the last war.'
WOMAN OVERHEARD IN A BUS, MASS OBSERVATION, 1945

The Troop formed up on the Square at St. John's Wood with 18-pounders for the first post-war Royal Salute in full dress, June 1946.

Coming into action, Hyde Park, 13 June 1946. Note the Nissen huts and flag pole of the military camp in the background,

As with much of the rest of London, St. John's Wood also suffered from the effects of the German blitz during the war. As well as the bomb that destroyed the mobilisation store in the barracks, All Saints Church in Queen's Terrace and Lord's Cricket Ground had all suffered some damage, and in 1944 a V1 flying bomb landed at the bottom of Ordnance Hill and destroyed a row of terraced houses. Robinsfield School now stands in this area today. These are just a few of the incidents that affected this leafy and near-suburban area of north London during six long years of war.

When the Riding Troop arrived from Shoeburyness the barracks had recently been vacated by the Signal Troop and, not surprisingly perhaps, was in a state of wartime disrepair. Much work needed to be done. Many of the men recruited for the new troop came from artillery regiments in Europe and some had served at the Wood before with such famous batteries as O, J and K, and their knowledge was invaluable at this time. All draught training and salute practices took place at Wormwood Scrubs, a training area used by the battery at the Wood for many years before the war and now, still with the Anti-Aircraft gun emplacements intact, an ideal site for the new troop to practise its driving skills and drills. Initially,

there were only enough horses from the Remount Depot at Melton Mowbray to provide four gun teams. The other two teams, complete with drivers, were provided by the Mounted Section of the Experimental Establishment at Shoeburyness and they also took part in the salute. The shortage of horses at the time precluded the use of mounted detachments, and for the first Royal Salute the detachments rode on the limbers. The situation was not helped perhaps by the fact that horse meat was used to supplement the national diet during the early post-war years.

As the Troop came into action in Hyde Park just before noon on 13 June it was hard to believe that some of those on parade had never ridden a horse until two months previously. One chap, Trumpeter Coward, was riding a large Skewbald, with a reputation for 'taking hold', which, in his rather inexperienced hands at the time, disappeared off down the park at a healthy gallop.

Once the salute was completed the Troop departed to Shoeburyness for three months training. By the middle of the following year the 18-pounders had been replaced by 13-pounders, found from various parts of the country, including two that were obtained from an Army Cadet Force unit in Manchester where they had been used to train the cadets at gun drill.

The King inspects the Riding Troop, now equipped with the more traditional 13-pounders, on the square during his visit to St. John's Wood Barracks, 24 October 1947.

Training for the musical drive began in 1947 and the first performance by the Riding Troop took place at Aldershot on 26 July. On 24 October the Troop were honoured with a visit by the King, the first such visit by a reigning monarch to St. John's Wood barracks. During his visit he inspected the Troop in full ceremonial order and watched a display of them coming into action on the square. Thereafter he began a tour of the barracks, including visits to Right Section stables as well as the Farrier's Shop, Gun Park and one of the barrack rooms. During the visit he was introduced to the BSM, WO2 Jackson, and Miss Sutton, who as Manageress had spent almost twenty years in charge of the NAAFI at the Wood. He then retired to the Officers' Mess where, upon signing the visitor's book, he crossed out the word 'Riding' and substituted 'King's'. The establishment of the Troop at the time was: five officers, 121 other ranks, 110 horses and six 13-pounders.

In February 1948, Miss Sutton retired and to mark the occasion she was presented with a gold bracelet with an enamelled RHA cipher mounted on it and the following inscription was inside: 'To Miss Sutton from grateful Horse Artillerymen, 1928–1948, M, J, F and K Batteries and the King's Troop RHA'. On her

death some time later the bracelet was bequeathed to the King's Troop and remains today in the silver room of the Sergeants' Mess.

On 19 April the Troop celebrated the second anniversary of its reformation—which actually fell on the 17 April, but as many were away racing or show jumping it was delayed by a few days. The Troop birthday would later be changed to 24 October, the day that the King gave them their title, but for the first few years the date in April was used. The day began with reveille at 6.30 a.m., (a welcome 'lie in' for most) and 'stables' and routine work were completed before breakfast so that the remainder of the day could be devoted to mounted sports.

The less serious races took place in the morning, starting with the 'ball and bucket' race—virtually a mounted potato race without saddles. Thereafter followed mounted wrestling teams of six with stable head collars and no saddles competing in a small arena with the object of dismounting their opponents or forcing them out of the ring. This was won by A Sub-section. And later the VC race again without saddles. The final event of the morning was the Old Soldier's race which was won by Sgt. Holmes.

After a fairly 'liquid lunch' the afternoon session

The Commanding Officer, Major J A Norman DSO RHA, leads the Troop back into barracks from a draught parade at Wormwood Scrubs, 1948. The main gates were still made of wood at that time.

began with recruits show jumping followed by the pair horse jumping, won by Sgt. Senior with Wendell and Wilkie. The final event was the Open Jumping which was won by Gunner Pierce on Watney, one of several German horses that the Troop had been given on their formation. The day finished with an all ranks dance in the dining hall. Troop birthday celebrations such as this and similar sporting events continued at the Wood until the late 1960s.

The first post-war musical drive by the King's Troop at Olympia was performed at the Royal Tournament in June 1948. The Gunner magazine reported the event thus:

'The most interesting event of regimental interest last month was the resuscitation of the Royal Horse Artillery drive at the Royal Tournament. It was a sporting effort on the part of Major Norman (the CO) to attempt it under the conditions prevailing, and all must agree that is has been abundantly justified. We are glad to learn that at the conclusion of the drive on the opening day the King personally congratulated the Troop on their performance'. From this fairly inauspicious beginning the Troop went on to perfect and perform the musical drive at Olympia and later Earls Court as well as many

venues in Europe and North America.

In June 1950 the annual Royal Tournament moved from Olympia to the Exhibition Building, Earls Court. The arena at Earls Court, being seven yards wider than that at Olympia, was better suited to the various tight manoeuvres of the musical drive and therefore ensured fewer accidents. Later that summer the Troop made its first visit to the Royal Norfolk Show at Lynn. The horses and guns were loaded on the special train provided by British Railways at Holloway and arrived at Wolferton Station on the Royal Estate at Sandringham four hours later, and just a few moments before the train carrying the Royal Family arrived from London. Whilst at the show the Troop was honoured by several informal visits from the King and Queen with the Princess Margaret They arrived without ceremony and with the King driving his own car. His Majesty remarked on the extreme youth of the soldiers taking part—National Service had begun the year before and most boys at age 18 and over were 'called up' for military service of 18 months to begin with. This was later increased to 2 years. During the early post-war years the King, who was Captain-General of the Royal Artillery, took a

The King's Troop enters the arena at the Royal Tournament, Olympia, 1949.

great interest in Regimental matters and in 1951 he decreed that the lines and acorns worn on the left breast of the RHA full dress jacket should be moved to the right side, so that those with 'his' campaign medals from the War should not be obscured.

Life in Britain was gradually returning to some kind of normality. A great programme of house building was in process and the reconstruction of city centres badly damaged by Hitler's bombs was progressing slowly. The barracks changed little during this period, the grime and smoke that blackened the barrack blocks and some of the other buildings were yet to be removed or painted over. Other parts of St. John's Wood were at a similar stage of decoration and repair.

On 6 February 1952 King George VI died at Sandringham and the Troop had the very sad task of providing the gun carriage that bore his body from Sandringham House to Wolferton Station, and, on arrival in London, from King's Cross to Westminster Hall. During the following week life at St. John's Wood was frenetic to say the least. Preparations began almost immediately with the collection from the Rotunda Museum of the two guns and limbers which had been used for previous State funerals

On Thursday 7 February the Troop fired a Royal Salute of 56 guns in Hyde Park—one round for every year of the Sovereign's life. The same afternoon the Troop was ordered to send the detachment, with officer, to Sandringham to carry the body of the King to Wolferton Station. On Friday 8 February the Troop marched out of the barracks for Hyde Park to fire a 41-gun salute marking the proclamation of the new Queen.

For the journey from King's Cross to Westminster Hall on Monday 11 February experience had shown that it was preferable to use the rubber-tyred 13-pounder gun carriage, as many parts of the route were still paved with stones. For the State funeral itself on Friday 15 February the Troop were once again in Hyde Park firing a 56-gun Salute whilst the cortège processed through the streets of London to Paddington Station. At 2 p.m. that day all ranks of the Troop, apart from those on duty for the final part of the ceremony at Windsor, joined a muster

Funeral of King George VI. The King's Troop carries the coffin of the King from Sandringham to Wolferton Station, February 1952.

parade on the barracks square, where in silence they paid their last respects to the King whom they had special cause to remember.

Much of the rest of that year was an anti-climax for Troop members but the show season kept them busy with appearances at the RA 'At Home' at Woolwich and at the Royal Tournament in June, where for the first time since before the War the Sword, Lance and Revolver competition was included and at which several members of the Troop took part.

By the early 1950s almost half of the Troop strength was made up of National Servicemen, thus there was a continuous turnover and training every two years. Some men came from racing yards or civilian stables and a few were quite accomplished in the equestrian world before being 'called up'. Their transition to the arduous life at the Wood was therefore much easier. At this time the Commanding Officer was Major Frank Weldon, who remained in command for almost five years. He was an accomplished horseman who, with his horse 'Kilbarry', was to represent Great Britain at the Olympic Games in Stockholm in 1956 where they won a team gold medal and an individual bronze.

At the coronation of the new Queen, Elizabeth II, in June 1953 the Troop formed part of the procession through London: this being only one of many commitments during the year, including gun salutes and performing the musical drive around the country.

Life at the Wood followed with much the same culture as before the Second World War with a daily routine and a disciplinary code to match. Reveille was at 6 a.m. and all men employed in the sub-sections had to be in their respective horse lines by 6.10 a.m.. Those detailed to ride on morning exercise then had 15 minutes to tack up their three horses before 'File out'

The Troop march past at the SSAFA Tattoo, White City, 1953.

sounded at 6.30 a.m.. During the week, morning exercise was invariably 'Dressed Exercise', so-called because soldiers had the comfort of a saddle to ride on. This normally lasted for an hour and half. On Saturdays, or when otherwise ordered, morning exercise lasted for just an hour, was ridden with a saddle blanket and surcingle, and was known as 'Rough Exercise'. Once morning exercise and the mucking out were complete the first parade of the day after breakfast was at 9 a.m.. Thereafter, the day followed a familiar pattern with morning stables parade at 11 a.m., normally taken by the BSM, or later, the RSM. At all parades the trumpeters (up to twelve on some occasions) would be assembled at the top of the square, next to the RSM, and on his command they would sound the relevant call, which could often be heard half way up Wellington Road.

On a normal working day the last parade would be the 4 p.m. stables parade when everyone would turn in for 'wisping' and to bed down the horses. Once the horses had filed out to water on the troughs and the feeds

Picket-mounting on the Regimental Square, 1954.

placed around each lines, the Orderly Trumpeter would sound 'feed up', and to the echo of a huge 'whinny' from the horses who recognised the call, feeds were placed in the mangers. For those detailed for night picket and other duties, the next parade would be Picket-Mounting at 6.10 p.m. preceded by the ceremony of 'Retreat' at 6p.m. when the Troop flag was ceremoniously lowered to the sound of the trumpet call. Anyone outside their barrack block or other building had to stand to attention until it was concluded—regardless of their state of dress or how occupied at the time. The final

Royal Horse Artillery Association parade and church service in the Riding School, October 1954.

call of the day was of course Last Post at 10 p.m., and as the notes of this melancholy call died away, a hush fell over the barracks square, broken only at various intervals during the night by the clatter of short rack chains against a manger or the occasional squeal from

a horse who has been bitten by his neighbour.

St. John's Wood barracks was not only the home of the saluting battery. As the last and only remaining RHA battery station it was also the recognised headquarters of the Royal Horse Artillery Association. On a very cold, snow-driven day in January 1954 a re-dedication ceremony was held at the barracks on the occasion of the blessing of a new Association Standard and to mark the re-titling of the Association from 'Old Comrades Association' to the present day RHA Association. This was a fairly large parade and service for the times, with soldiers from both the King's Troop and 3rd RHA taking part, as well as one hundred and twenty members and families of the Association. The parade took place on the barracks square with a drumhead service in the Riding School and lunch thereafter in the various Messes. The barracks remained the 'home headquarters' of the Association until 2012.

Major Frank Weldon, who commanded the Troop for almost five years, and the British three-day event team, which won a team gold medal and Major Weldon an individual bronze medal at the Olympic Games, at Melbourne, 1956.

Top-left The drivers each with a pair of horses from the gun teams undergo instruction in the outdoor manège.

Above: A regimental 'Open Day' at the barracks in 1956 and a Royal Salute, which the families were invited to attend.

By the mid 1950s the relatively 'new' King's Troop had become a firmly established part of the ceremonial heart of London with the Household Troops. Despite the continual turnover of National Servicemen they managed to maintain—and in many cases improve—upon the standards that the RHA was so famous for. Not only were members of the Troop becoming very successful in the various equestrian competitions of the time: they were consolidating their reputation as professional horsemen. The musical drive in particular went from strength to strength and the show seasons became ever busier as the Troop's fame spread far and wide. A good indication of life at the time was recorded in Gunner magazine in early 1956.

'What a great year (1955) it has been for the Troop. Sunshine practically non-stop and the busiest show season from May to October for some long time. It started in May with the Woolwich 'At Home'. We then

An overview of the section stables at the barracks.

galloped through a sea of mud at Aldershot before going on to three weeks at the Royal Tournament. During this period we fired the usual salutes for the Queen's Birthday Parade and other important events in the annual ceremonial calendar. At the tournament we had much success when winning the Services Team Jumping competition and for the first time since 1902 we had in Lance Bombardier Elliott of F Sub-section, the first Gunner winner of the Sword, Lance and Revolver competition. Lance-Bombardier Elliott is a National Serviceman who will return to the Lancashire Constabulary next year from whence he came on being 'called up'.

'Straight from Earls Court we loaded onto a special train which, in glorious summer weather, took us to Norwich for the Norfolk Show, on to Nottingham for the Royal Show and up to Harrogate for the Great Yorkshire Show. Broiling sun, sweating horses, huge, cheering crowds, Scotch salmon and cold turkey, and some grand drives, marred only by

THE KING'S TROOP 63

The King's Troop at Admiralty Arch during the Coronation procession, 2 June 1953.

a new and rough ground at Harrogate which shook us by turning over a couple of guns. Great fun it all was, and wherever we went old Gunners turned up to cheer us on and cast a knowing eye over the horses and guns.

'In August we went to Ogbourne St. George for our annual camp, and still the sun shone. We shot on their rifle range, read maps (with varying success) by day and night, fought miniature but highly mobile wars over the surrounding country—the Marlborough Downs, Savernake Forest and the Vale of Pewsey, washed London smog from lungs and heart— Sergeant Walker's in particular, for his A Sub-section won the shield by a distance. From Marlborough to Woolwich dropping off en route to gallop round the ring of a delightful little one-day show at Newbury.

The section horse lines virtually unchanged since they were built in 1870.

Instructional Rides and training in the outdoor manège. The Recruits Ride.

Our chief memory of the Woolwich Tattoo is getting very wet and being scared stiff but inspired beyond words by the most terrific reception that the Troop has ever had. Then the Drive on the Saturday night

A remount is put through its paces during loose jumping.

with the Master Gunner taking the salute, the RHA Association packing the stands, and four of our six lead drivers singing their swan songs. It had to be good—it was.'

Show seasons and summer camps such as this, busy, and with endless journeys by rail to all parts of the country, continued in much the same way until the rolling stock for the transport of horses and cattle was scrapped by British Rail in the early 1970s.

One other popular event at the barracks at this time was the Open Day for families and parents. Taking advantage of the Queen's Birthday for 1956 falling on a Saturday for the first time in many years, invitations were sent to all parents to come up to London to see the salute, have lunch and tea in the barracks and take a look round. A total of 350 turned up! Fortunately it was a beautiful day and the party gathered at the barracks at 10.30 a.m. to see the parade. Directly the Troop moved off, the parents were marshalled into seven double-decker buses and taken down to Hyde Park. On return to the barracks lunch was served in one sitting in the Riding School with the RA Mounted Band playing from the gallery. The afternoon was spent walking around the barracks and stables and after tea the guests left for home.

The Defence Review in 1957 and the decision a short time later to end National Service by early 1962 brought about a great deal of change to the life and culture of the Troop. During the years of National Service discipline was very strict and the code of conduct for dress and behaviour both in and out of barracks was rigidly maintained. Dress for walking out and weekend leave was invariably Service Dress or smart civilian clothes which for those with long journeys ahead of them was an uncomfortable prospect. To get around this, many used The Prince of Wales pub, which was on the corner of the cross roads of Ordnance Hill and Queen's Grove to change into civilian clothes. This pub was known locally as 'Rosie's', the name of the landlady, who took a motherly interest in the 'boys' at the barracks and allowed them to use a room at the side of the establishment as a changing room. In the 1960s the pub was replaced with a trendy establishment known as the 'Rossetti'. That too has now given way to a new apartment block.

The last National Serviceman walked through the gates of St. John's Wood barracks in early 1960. Thereafter the recruiting programme for the new regular army gathered pace and by 1963 all but those few who had signed on for an extra year or more remained. In November 1962 the Troop was honoured once again with a royal visit. On this occasion it was Her Majesty The Queen making her first visit to the Troop at the Wood. This was a very popular event for everybody, including the local residents who turned out in great numbers to see the Queen arrive and depart. For this occasion Troop personnel were dressed in the 'new' Service Dress with collar and tie which, over the next two years replaced the old pre-war vintage box collar form of Service Dress and knee puttees.

By any standards, 1964 was a remarkable year at the Wood. In April the Annual Administrative Parade took the form of a full-blown mounted review and

A common sight in the Spring and Summer months: grooming at the side of the stables.

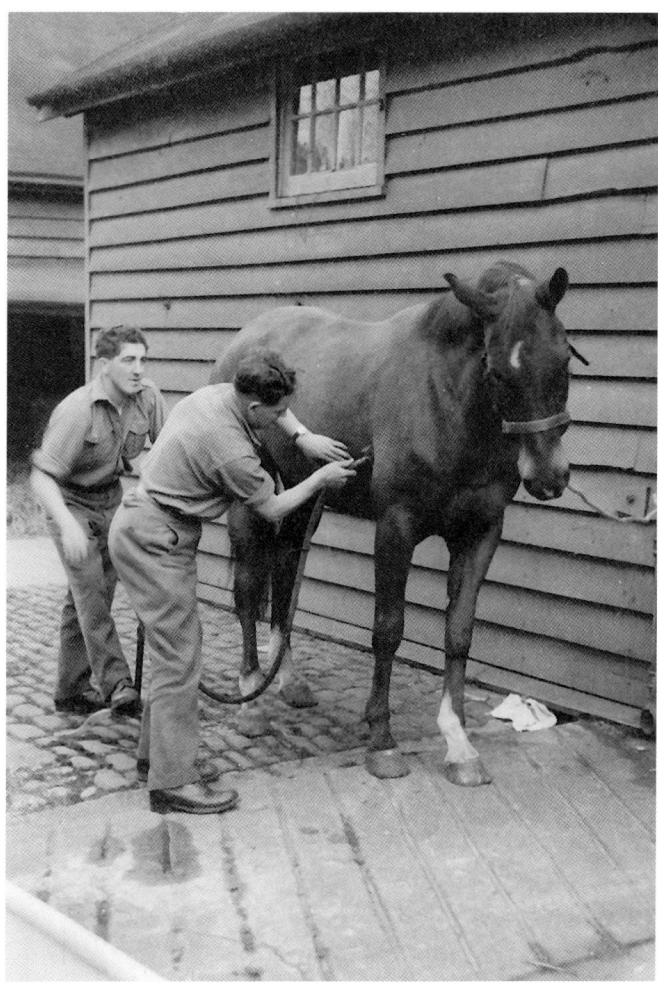
'Watchman', a much loved charger, takes a keen interest in the soldiers delegated to clip him using the cumbersome hand-powered clippers of the period.

gallop-past in Regents' Park, the first such parade since before the Second World War. Rehearsals for this great event began as ever at Wormwood Scrubs, and only moved to the parade area on Cumberland Green a week or two before the event. For the parade there was much sunshine, large crowds and the park trees were covered in spring blossom. To compliment this wonderful setting the parade went off extremely well and the Troop marched back to barracks via Avenue Road and Norfolk Road with its reputation greatly enhanced.

The hounds of the Royal Artillery Hunt being exercised in the manège during a visit to the barracks.

Wagtail enjoys a splash in the troughs.

Watering on the troughs. This ritual took place three times daily, usually before each feed and on return from morning exercise. The horses loved it. They could drink as much as they liked and splash about and make waves—just like children! Their temperament and utter reliability had, no doubt, much to do with their origins, as most were bred in Ireland.

Wallace and Charlie, two favourite characters en route to Woolwich.

At this time the annual calendar of Troop events always included a period during the training season normally from late September until early April, when the new horses, called 'Remounts' in military terms, were collected from the veterinary corps depot at Melton Mowbray. For the first ten weeks the remounts were broken and trained to basic level by the Equitation Sergeant aided by a specially selected group of riders from each subsection. Invariably this training took place uninterrupted at either Aldershot or Colchester.

In September, for the first time in its history, the Troop travelled abroad to perform the musical drive at the British Trade exhibition in Copenhagen. Moving horses by air was in its infancy at this time and the Troop's move of sixty animals over three days was, at the time, the biggest shipment of horses in air history. The week of departure in mid September, saw almost night and day activity at the Wood. Two parties of horses left each day, the first at 4.30 a.m.. Boarding the propeller-driven DC6 aircraft at Gatwick provided yet another challenge. These aircraft could carry ten horses, two abreast with very little spare room. The

Harrowing the perimeter track on the square. A daily chore, with the horse usually provided by the Orderly Sergeant's own Sub-section. 1956.

A drive practice at the 'slips', an ash covered car park at Regents Park, much used by the Troop until it was given a hardened surface in the 1960s.

easiest way to load them it was discovered was by each man leading a horse up a long ramp and into the aircraft. Apart from some slight concern on take off and landing the horses were perfectly behaved throughout the journey.

The British Tattoo was performed twice nightly, at 6.45 p.m. and 9.30 p.m. for a fortnight in the beautiful setting of the Danish Life Guards square, with floodlit Rosenborg Castle providing a splendid background. The guns and harness were kept in the arena area; the horses and men were accommodated two miles away in the Danish Hussars Staging Barracks stables. This was a great experience for all ranks and it brought the show season to an enjoyable climax. On return to the Wood in mid-October everyone was plunged straight into the annual training cycle and the inevitable ceremonial duties of the autumn period.

As if all this excitement were not enough, the Troop had two representatives in the British Olympic Three-Day Event team competing in Tokyo: Sergeant Ben Jones with Master Bernard and Captain James Templer—a former Centre Section Commander who had recently left the Troop—with his horse M' Lord Connolly. Though neither got into the medals they both acquitted themselves well.

As a result of the success of the British Trade exhibition in Denmark in 1964, the British Import Union decided to organise another in Milan, Italy, the following September. Before this took place, however, an outbreak of Equine Flu spread throughout Britain

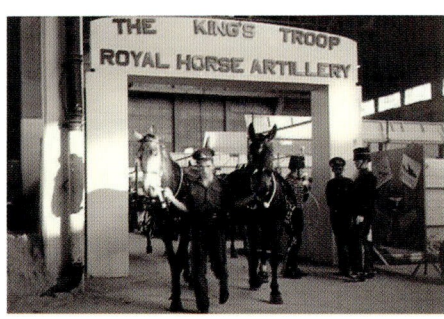

Scenes from the Royal Tournament, Earls Court. **Clockwise from above:** The march past at the end of the musical drive; The Troop Gun Park; Filing out from the stables; The harness and saddlery prepared for display to the public at the end of the show; The public visiting the horse lines after the show; The horse lines.

A pastel painting by Joan Wanklyn of the Queen in Right Section Lines during her visit to the Troop in November 1962.

in the early spring of 1965, resulting in the cancellation of most of the planned show season. During this period, which lasted until the end of May, the daily routine at the Wood included walking the horses in pairs to Regents Park in the morning sunshine for an hour grazing, a rare treat for the horses and a welcome change for the men.

As soon as the horses were pronounced fit they were back in training for the Royal Tournament, immediately after which the Troop entrained at Kensington Olympia for Liverpool and a military tattoo in Waverley Park. The most notable aspect of this show was the rain, which came down in buckets for almost every performance.

Once back at the Wood the Troop made ready to fly to Milan, on this occasion courtesy of British Caledonian Airways and Bristol Britannia aircraft. All troops taking part in the Tattoo were accommodated in a local Italian Army artillery barracks, named, appropriately, Santa Barbara Caserna (Saint Barbara being the Patron Saint of all Artillerymen). The accommodation was very basic

but acceptable, and the Troop had a very enjoyable time, despite being routed in a show jumping competition against a team from the Italian Army, two of whom (the d'Inzeo brothers) were members of the Italian Olympic team. On conclusion of the

The Queen meets Left Section horses during her first visit to the Troop at St. John's Wood, November 1962.

B Sub-section team lead the Troop into the musical drive at the Bath and West Show, Taunton, 1963.

During the creation of the underground car-park at Hyde Park, the saluting base for gun salutes was moved to a temporary location on the south west side of the park a few hundred metres from the Serpentine. Here they came into action with four guns only.

Arrival at Copenhagen airport for the British Trade Week Tattoo.

The Troop fire for the 1812 Overture during the finale of the British Trade Week Tattoo in Copenhagen, October 1964.

The Troop in action in St. James's Park firing the Minute Guns for the State Funeral of Sir Winston Churchill, January 1965.

A silhouette of the Troop at morning exercise on Hampstead Heath, 1966.

A remount being introduced to harness during section training on the main square, 1966.

The Troop fires a salvo at the conclusion of the display at a very wet Royal Highland Show, 1966.

tattoo all members of the Troop were treated to a few days 'R and R' which included trips to the Italian Alps. The author can remember enjoying lunch at a roadside café on a beautiful sunlit day amid the spectacular scenery on the shores of Lake Como.

In 1966 the Royal Artillery celebrated the 250th anniversary of its formation with a large parade on Horseguards at which the Troop took the lead. This was also a year during which the Troop travelled the length and breadth of the country performing at shows as far afield as Windsor and Edinburgh, then hacking to Glasgow for a show at Bellahouston Park before returning south for the Royal Tournament. Thereafter it was off by military train to Okehampton in Devon for Troop and Section Camps.

On 10 May 1967 history was made when the Troop took centre stage at the largest mounted parade to be held in the country since the war,

The Troop horses return from Regents Park where they had some welcome grazing during the Equine Flu epidemic, May 1965.

One of the Troop 13-pounder guns being used as a backdrop for a fashion shoot at the barracks in 1966.

Royal Review and Parade for King Faisal and HM The Queen, Hyde Park, May 1967.

Her Majesty The Queen, accompanied by King Faisal of Saudi Arabia reviewed the King's Troop in Hyde Park. The first rehearsal for this momentous event took place, as ever, at Wormwood Scrubs on a seasonally cold morning at the end of March. After many more early morning trips to the Scrubs, the first rehearsal with bands at Hyde Park took place at the end of April. As a result of bad weather, which blighted most of the days in the early part of spring, this proved to be the last, and on Monday 8 May the Troop marched out of barracks to fire a 41-gun salute to mark the arrival of King Faisal. Fortunately

The Troop returns to barracks at the conclusion of the Annual Administrative Inspection, 1966.

the weather was bright and dry and the salute went off without a hitch. Wednesday 10 May turned out to be a beautiful warm day full of sunshine and bright hats, all of which was recorded on film and by the outside broadcast service of the BBC. After the inspection and many intricate manoeuvres during the parade, the Troop came into action in front of the dais and fired one round Troop fire followed by one round Salvo. Thereafter they formed up in front of the dais, gave a Royal Salute at which the National Anthems were played, and the parade came to its conclusion.

This Royal Review was not the only notable event during the year, for at the conclusion of a busy show season at home, the Troop travelled to North America in September to take part in the World Horse Spectacular at EXPO 67 in Montreal, Canada. The Troop were flown across the Atlantic courtesy of Air France—which for the advance party meant a morning staging stop at Orly Airport, Paris, and a typically French breakfast. The horses were transported in Boeing 707s, loaded in pallets of three with a total of twenty-seven animals per aircraft. The horses and guns were accommodated at the showground with the officers and men at a local Royal Canadian Army Ordnance Corps barracks on the outskirts of the city. For this show the Troop performed the Earls Court drive and then came into action, with dismounted

A gun slides and tips over during a very wet Press Day rehearsal at Wormwood Scrubs in March 1967. Whilst accidents such as this were not exactly rare, neither were they that common. All was well in the end and nobody—equine or human, was injured.

Clockwise from top: Loading the horses at Heathrow for Montreal and EXPO 67; The action at the end of the display; The 'Scissors' movement toward the end of the drive; The Troop rehearses the musical drive in the Automotive Stadium, Montreal.

detachments, much the same as in Copenhagen three years earlier. As with similar such shows, there was a short period of 'R and R' at the end which allowed members of the Troop some sightseeing of the World Trade Exhibition site which was located on a man-made island in the middle of the St. Lawrence River.

The penultimate year for the Troop in the old barracks was marked by continuing success in the world of three-day-eventing when SSgt. Ben Jones, the Troop Equitation Instructor, was selected to ride for Britain at the Mexico Olympics on a horse loaned for the event, called the 'Poacher'. Despite torrential rain and floods during the cross-country phase of the event, SSgt. Jones finished the course in fine style to clinch the team gold medal for Britain. There was much celebration and a rapturous welcome for him on his return to the Wood that year.

Top: A much more enjoyable Press Day at Wormwood Scrubs, 1968.

Right: The Royal Tournament 1969. The Lines horses, wearing their special Earls Court Dust Sheets, prepare to file on to the water trough at lunchtime.

The Trumpeters sound the opening fanfare for the musical drive at the Royal Tournament, 1968.

The British Three-Day-Event team, gold medallists at the Mexico Olympics, 1968, including Staff Sergeant Ben Jones of the King's Troop.

Preparation for the Troop's departure from the Wood gathered pace in the early new year of 1969. Many visits were made to Combermere Barracks at Windsor to finalise the details of accommodation for horses and men as well as a special training area for the musical drive. The latter was created just off the Long Walk, almost in the castle grounds, and normal draught training and salute practices took place in Windsor Great Park. At the conclusion of yet another busy show season and ceremonial duties, the Troop packed up and began the historic move to Windsor. By the end of September the last vestiges of their existence at the barracks had been removed or destroyed and the Wood lay empty for the first time since 1946. The married families remained in Jubilee Buildings or at Bracknell Lodge in Hampstead, and commuted each morning to Windsor. 1969 not only marked the end of a golden decade for the King's Troop, travelling as they had to many parts of the world to perform the musical drive, it also marked the end of an era and a culture that was destined never to be restored.

Top: One of the many 'VIP' visits to the Troop. Here the Section Commanders and the Numbers One are assembled in the Gun Park for the presentation of the Long Service and Good Conduct medal to the REME Artificer Staff Sergeant.

Bottom: Demolition 1970. The riding school stands alone and abandoned amid the rubble of the stable lines and old married quarters.

Troop Camp

Unlike the saluting batteries stationed at St. John's Wood before the Second World War, the 'new' King's Troop ceased to be recognised as an operational gun battery in 1951. Thus, the requirement for normal military training was carried out at the annual Troop Camp which took place usually in July or August each year and over the years has been held in a variety of locations throughout the country, including military camps and training areas at Ogbourne St. George on the Marlborough Downs in Wiltshire, Okehampton, Norfolk, Folkestone and on at least one occasion, the North Yorkshire coast. Until the early 1960s the guns were also taken to camp and the annual shooting tests and other military training were carried out at the same time. At every camp, however, inter sub-section competitions, including team and individual show jumping, cross-country and gymkhana events were keenly fought over by the sub-sections. The following pages contain snapshots from some of the camps during this period.

Loading the horses at Holloway for Harrogate, 1954. These were cattle trucks, known colloquially as 'Oxfits' and used for the gun team horses (known as Lines horses). The officers' chargers went in the racehorse boxes when available, as did the more difficult or nervous Lines animals.

The annual personal shooting tests all soldiers had to complete.

The Troop Hunter Trials.

The VC race, a popular Gymkhana event much enjoyed by horses and soldiers alike.

A water halt at Heathrow airport en-route to camp at Twesledown in the 1950s.

The section horse lines where the horses are out in the open and tethered centrally with a shackle rope on one hind leg to prevent kicking. They wore heavy jute rugs at night or waterproof rugs during inclement weather.

Gun Team Pairs Jumping.

The prize-giving ceremony, where it was customary for the Commanding Officer's wife to present the rosettes and trophies.

Chapter Six

SUNSET—
A NEW BARRACKS AND A
SAD FAREWELL

1971–2012

Demolition of the old buildings began in early 1970, and after more than two years of commuting from Windsor to London for State ceremonial, the King's Troop marched in to the new barracks on 17 April 1972. During the rebuild virtually the whole of the camp had been demolished except for the Officers' Mess building and the ancient riding school, the interior of which was now restored to its original dimensions. Whilst there were some advantages with the new barracks, there were also many problems, some of which were never to be resolved before its ultimate demolition some 40 years later. Added to this were the inevitable changes to the structure and composition of the Army which, by the dawn of the new millennium, had changed the culture and traditions of the saluting battery almost beyond recognition.

'We may our ends by our beginnings know'
Sir John Denham, *Of Prudence*, 1668

The march back into St. John's Wood Barracks began from the old Victorian cavalry barracks at Albany Street, in Regents Park, which had been used throughout the Troop's stay at Windsor as the mounting base for all ceremonial events in London. Before the march-in, much of the stores and equipment from Windsor, and all personnel and horses not required for the parade, had been returned to the Wood. All that remained was for the Troop itself to march through the gates of the new barracks.

Preparations for the march-in began as usual at the very early hour of 5.30 a.m. when the Troop departed from Windsor by horse box and pantechnicon. On arrival at Regents Park Barracks they unloaded horses, harness and guns, and after the usual preparations, formed up on the ancient square for the last time. With the Commanding Officer leading, the Troop set off in column of route for St. John's Wood. Fortunately, it was a dry and bright spring day and on arrival at the barracks they were greeted by the customary Sword Guard and a large crowd of local residents as well as several hundred of the Troop's families. As the new barrack square was somewhat smaller than the previous one, the Troop formed up facing north toward the Section Lines.

The layout of the new barracks was quite different from that which had existed before 1969. Though one could argue that the old barracks evolved in a haphazard manner, driven as much by military and political expedience as any desire to create a logical or

The GOC London District inspects the Troop on return to St. John's Wood Barracks, 17 April 1972.

practical home for the residents, the previous layout had at least made the most use of the small area that was available. No such thing could be said of the new plan. In the old layout most of the main buildings were spread around the perimeter of the barracks, with a central open area dominated by the parade square and exercise track. The new barracks had most of the buildings set forward from the perimeter, thus very much reducing the size of the main square, which was also, unfortunately, dominated by a three story high angular and very unattractive barrack block. The maintenance of these buildings and the exercise track around the square were to prove troublesome over the next forty years.

On 21 April a Regimental Open Day was held to show off the new barracks to the families and the people of St. John's Wood. Shortly afterwards, the Troop set off on the annual show season and the familiar round of ceremonial duties in the capital and at Windsor. To mark their return to the new barracks, the Troop was visited by Her Majesty the Queen on 6 June 1972. As with her previous visit in 1962 there was a large crowd of local residents and married families to greet her on arrival at Ordnance Hill. After an extensive tour of the barracks, visiting every department including, of course, the stables, Her Majesty took luncheon in the Officers' Mess with the Master Gunner and the officers of the Troop.

For the remainder of the year the Troop calendar was packed with military and civilian shows as well as the normal ceremonial duties. The show season culminated in August with the United

Loading the horses for one of the last rail moves of the Troop (on this occasion from Aldershot to Harrogate).

Counties Show at Carmarthen, South Wales. As British Rail had sold off or scrapped most of its rolling stock for the transportation of horses and cattle, the journey to this far flung part of Wales was carried out largely by road with only the gun team horses travelling by rail. This was the final occasion when the Troop was to travel anywhere by rail. The following year the last of the rolling stock had gone and transportation to any part of the United Kingdom would now be by road alone.

The following year brought the most radical change to the ceremonial duties of the saluting battery when, for the first time in their history, they marched past Her Majesty the Queen at Buckingham Palace on the conclusion of the Queen's Birthday Salute and the 'Trooping the Colour' ceremony on Horse Guards Parade. Before this however, there was the Annual Administrative Parade for the General Officer Commanding London District which took place annually during the month of April. The parade was normally held at Regents Park (although on very wet occasions it was held in Hyde Park) and was the precursor to the ceremonial and show calendar. Before the parade for the GOC there was often a full dress rehearsal at which the Director Royal Artillery took the salute. These occasions were an opportunity for the local residents to see at very close quarters the Troop at their best, and many hundreds of people made the short journey down to Regents Park to watch the parade.

A few months later, on 4 September 1973, a much more historic event took place when the Troop provided the Queen's Life Guard at Whitehall. The rationale for this historic decision was given at the time as a good opportunity

A composite half-battery from the Troop fires a salute on the Maifeld, in front of the Berlin Olympic Stadium during a press day display for the British Berlin Tattoo, 1971.

'Bobby', No 32 of A Sub-section, decides to try the sandwiches during a refreshment break at the Charlottenburg Palace, Berlin, 1971.

Top:
An aerial view of the musical drive at the Tidworth Military Tattoo, 1971.

Centre: The Queen inspects Centre Section during her visit to the new barracks, June 1972.

Bottom:
The Queen at the Gun Park 1972.

to raise the profile of the Troop in the eyes of the general public and perhaps of some other, more influential people. Whether that actually came to pass is of course, a matter of conjecture. What is certain is that the King's Troop lost forever an important window in the annual calendar which hitherto had been used for troop camp and summer leave. Thereafter life became a little more complicated, and a certain amount of flexibility was lost.

For the soldiers the chance to take on a role performed almost exclusively by the Household Cavalry for several hundred years was a challenge to relish. The Troop approached this duty with its usual enthusiasm and vigour. Each section provided a Guard, A from Right Section, B from Centre Section and C from Left Section. The competition between each guard was fierce, as indeed it was among individuals to secure the privilege of being awarded the duty of mounted box sentry. After three weeks of intensive training on the square by the RSM, they were ready for the big day. On 4 September 'A' Guard arrived at Whitehall as the clock chimed 11 a.m.—perfect timing. There they formed up opposite the old guard from the Life Guards and after a few minutes of ceremonial ritual the King's Troop assumed responsibility for the Queen's Life Guard and in doing so wrote a new chapter in the history of the Royal Horse Artillery.

The 1970s was a turbulent decade for the Army, heavily engaged as it was with the campaign in Northern Ireland. This also had an impact on the security arrangements in the rest of the United Kingdom and resulted in military displays and tattoos taking much greater precautions when admitting the public to any area where military personnel lived or worked. Unfortunately the heightened security situation affected the Royal Tournament in particular and the age-old tradition of members of the public visiting the horse lines and other areas 'behind the scenes' at the end of the daily shows came to an end. Thus was lost another small piece of national and military tradition and culture, not to mention the pleasure that so many derived from such close contact with people and organisations normally only seen on television or in the newspapers. This tightening of security affected also the barracks at St. John's Wood and the immediate area, where restricted parking, CCTV and other security measures were installed and implemented.

During the decade the Troop continued to travel throughout the country performing at agricultural shows and tattoos, and occasionally there would be an event somewhere on the continent. The British Berlin Tattoo, at which the Troop first performed in 1971, became a fairly regular fixture every three or four years, and in 1975 the Troop took part in a military tattoo in Paris: their first ever performance in France. While there they were fortunate enough to be included in the march down the magnificent Champs Élysées.

Top: Queen's Birthday Parade, 1973. This was the very first occasion when the Troop ranked past Her Majesty at the Palace.

Centre:
A Long Guard provided by Centre Section forms up in the main courtyard at Horse Guards prior to being relieved by the new Guard from Left Section.

Bottom: A mounted Guard found by Centre Section during the very first occasion that the Troop provided the Queen's Life Guard at Whitehall, August 1973.

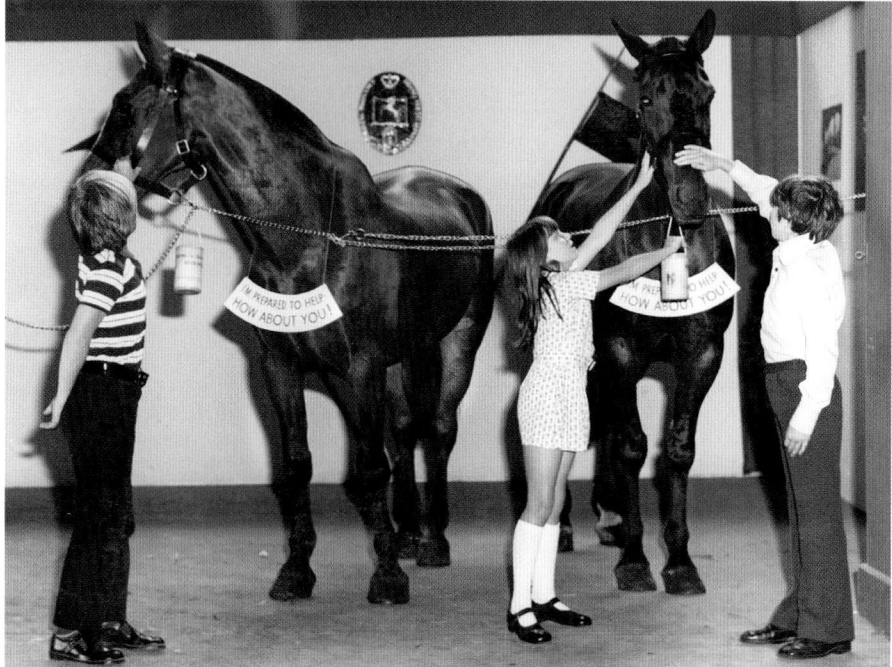

Top: The ARMEX show 1975, the conclusion of the display.

Left: The horses assist with a collection for the Riding for the Disabled at the Royal Tournament, 1974.

Bottom-left: The Lord Mayor of Westminster meets the horses during an informal visit to the barracks, 1975.

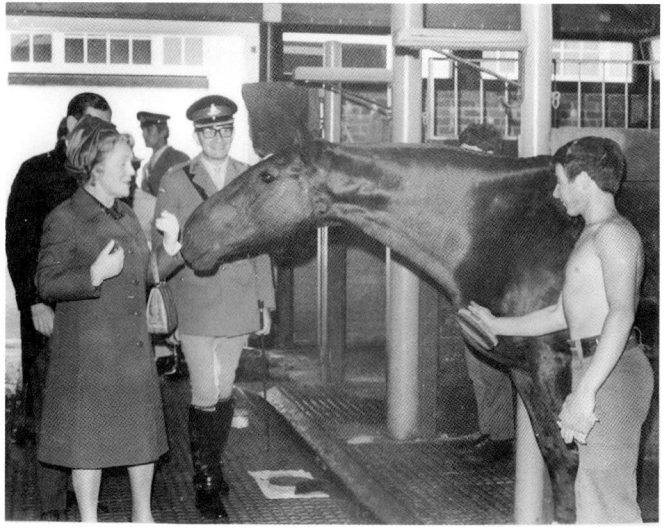

In 1977 Her Majesty The Queen celebrated her silver jubilee and as one might expect, the saluting battery had an important role in the celebrations, which included a procession through the streets of London, culminating at the Mall and Buckingham Palace. Shortly after this great event a national Firemen's Strike in the autumn resulted in St. John's Wood Barracks being turned into a Fire Station for almost three months, with scores of soldiers billeted in the Gun Park and several of the Army's ancient Green Goddess fire engines parked on the main square. Instead of the clatter of hooves and the sound of the trumpet to awaken the residents of St. John's Wood each morning there was the clanging

The Queen Mother's first visit to the troop—1978.

Training for the annual Remembrance Day Service at the Cenotaph. Here the Commanding Officer carries out a tailoring inspection.

Skill at Arms training in the Riding School.

The Queen Mother in Right Section horses lines.

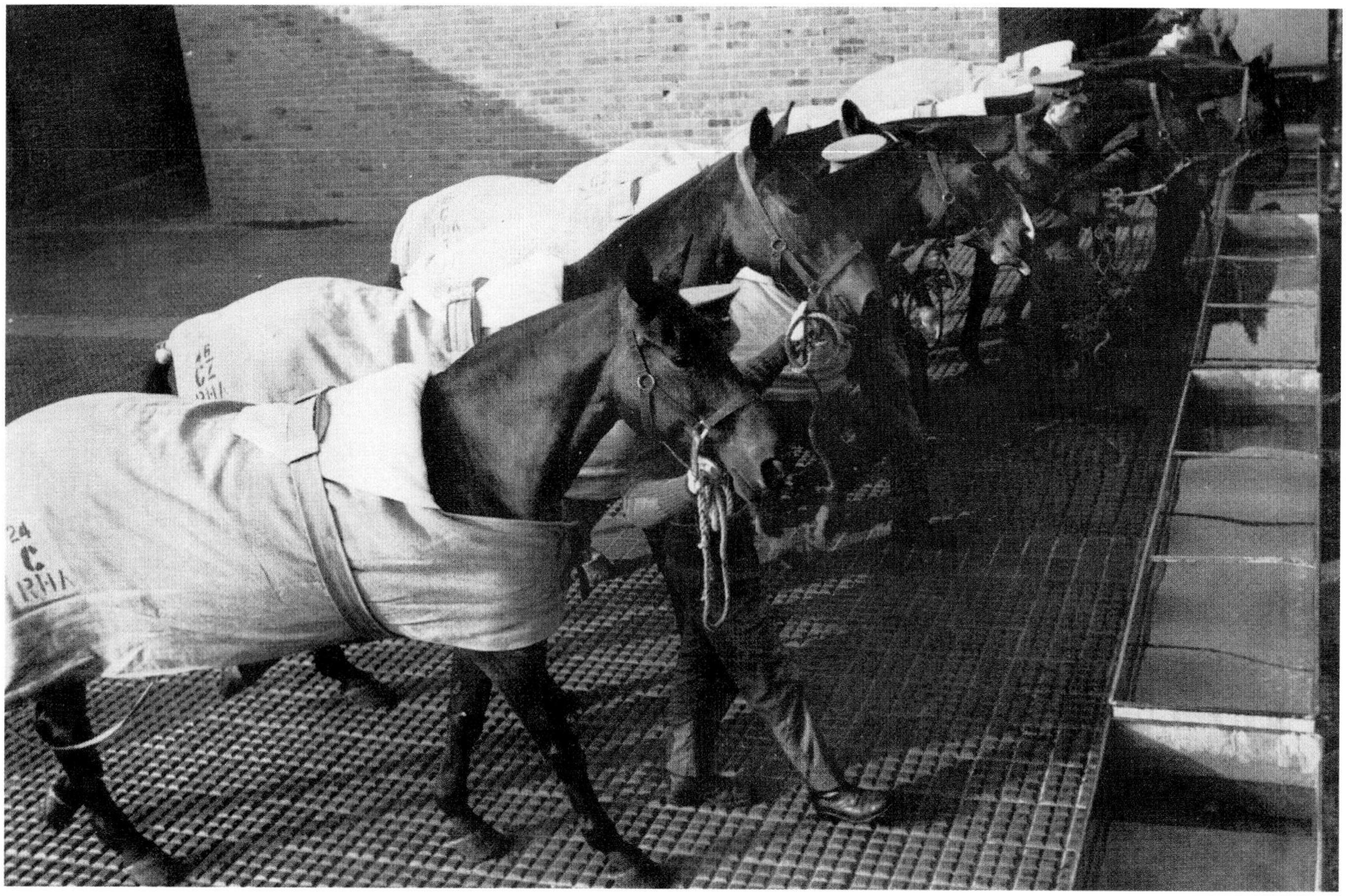

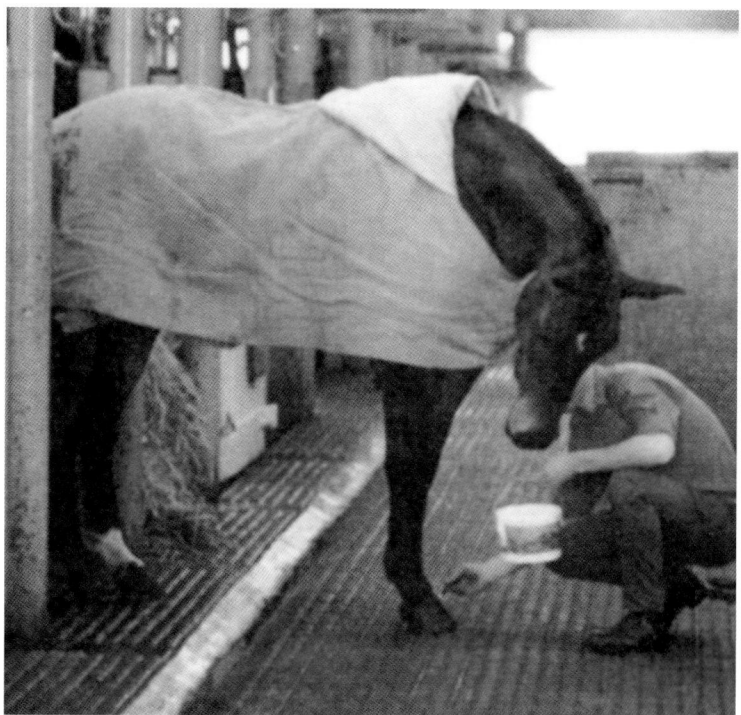

of ancient bells and klaxon horns from the old fire engines as they raced off down Ordnance Hill to answer yet another emergency call for help. This situation lasted for several months and finally came to an end in January 1978.

By the end of the decade much of the culture and routine of the Troop and the barracks had changed, driven in part by the prevailing security situation and the many other varied demands upon the Army has a whole. One of the reasons behind this change had been the decision at the end of the 1970s to allocate an operational role to the Troop in the event of war. The new role was to provide two Home Defence Companies for the protection of strategic and essential key points and services in and around London. Preparation for this role was fitted in to the already very busy training period in January and February of each year.

One of the other cultural casualties of the period and the interregnum caused by the rebuild was the 'Christmas routine'. Each Christmas Day the officers and Senior

Top: The watering ritual of using the troughs continued for some time in the new barracks.

Bottom: 'Sequin' takes an interest in the oiling up of her hooves at the end of the grooming period.

NCOs mucked out the horses whilst the Commanding Officer and the RSM took 'Gunfire'—tea or coffee laced with rum, around the barrack rooms for the soldiers, who were of course, still in bed (some recovering, badly, from the festivities of the previous night). Thereafter the Officers and SNCOS invariably had breakfast in the Sergeants' Mess. At 10 a.m. the Commanding Officer, Adjutant and the Troop Captain began to visit the families, most of whom lived behind the barracks in Jubilee Buildings. A drink was taken at each stop, the trick for the officers being not to get drunk! This could be a difficult task given the reputation of some of the Senior NCOs. At midday the officers entertained the Sergeants' Mess to drinks in the Officers' Mess and then all went to the Cook House to serve Christmas Dinner to the soldiers, which was preceded by the trumpeters sounding Christmas Dinner, one of the most difficult trumpet calls of the day—especially after a few drinks! Thereafter

Top: The first visit of HRH Princess Anne with her husband Captain Mark Phillips, 1982.

Bottom: The Princess in Centre Section lines.

The Queen's Life Guard, 1983. An immaculate turnout from the bays of Right Section.

The Guard Commander adjusts a soldier's dress before posting the mounted 'Box Men' at Whitehall.

The annual potential NCOs' course, being inspected on the square by the Commanding Officer.

Draught training at Wormwood Scrubs. By the early 1980s a small area at the east end of the common had been set aside for the use of the Troop.

the officers and Senior NCOs drank the health of the soldiers and then served the lunch.

Despite the requirement to provide the Queen's Life Guard each year, the Troop has been able to continue the traditional practice of annual camp, preferably somewhere near to the sea. Although rarely taken in July or August—September being more convenient after the summer block leave period—they managed to get away to some fairly remote places in either the West Country or perhaps a little further north where they are able to give the horses a break from the urban life of London and to practise some cross-country training and mounted sports, all of which are enjoyed immensely by both horses and men.

In 1981 the riots in Brixton provoked yet more restrictions on the security of the barracks, and the

situation became much worse in 1982 when the IRA attacked the Household Cavalry Life Guard as it marched through Hyde Park to its duties in Whitehall, killing several horses and soldiers. Simultaneously they exploded a bomb under the band of the Royal Green Jackets in Regents Park which killed eight bandsmen. The explosion from this attack was heard by everyone at the Wood. To counter these attacks the perimeter of the barracks was embellished with a very sharp rotating security grill and the daily exercise routine of departing the barracks at 6.30 a.m. was now carried out at varied timings. The problem of radio-controlled bombs such as that used against the cavalry was countered by the wearing of special apparatus, designed to interrupt electronic transmissions, by the rear-mounted man on all mounted parades and exercises. Ironically all this civil unrest coincided with the Royal Wedding of Prince Charles to Lady Diana Spencer. Part of the celebrations for this event included a firework display and concert in Hyde Park at which the Troop provided guns as accompaniment to the music.

Life at this time was not all gloom, and for some members of the Troop there came a ray of sunshine when a Section complete with gun detachments and the Troop trumpeters was invited to take part in the 'Festival of the Horse' in Atlantic City, USA. This great adventure began in early September 1982 when the horses, guns and men were loaded onto a Boeing 747 at London Heathrow airport on a normal scheduled flight. Little did the several hundred civilian passengers realise that behind a special screen half way down the aircraft there were forty or more horses munching away at their haynets in blissful ignorance of their surroundings. Despite this being a new experience the horses travelled the Atlantic like veterans of the sky, only displaying any interest in proceedings during the descent into the airport, when pricked ears and wide eyes suggested that this was not just a case of trapped wind!

The following year found the Troop once more performing at the British Berlin Tattoo. On this occasion only the personnel travelled by air; the

Queens' Life Guard, 1992 A splendid view of the Guard wearing the Troop's new saddle blankets. This photograph took pride of place on the front page of Gunner magazine that year.

The first visit of HRH Prince Charles and Diana, Princess of Wales to the Troop, 1985.

The Prince and Princess are given a demonstration of harness fitting.

During Section training it was not uncommon to see gun teams exercising in and around St. John's Wood and the Regents Park area.

horses and guns made the journey by land and sea. Although the show calendar remained busy it was becoming increasingly difficult and expensive to get to the bigger horse and agricultural shows. Military tattoos were also on the wane. Only the larger tattoos such as Aldershot and Edinburgh continued on a regular basis, and of course, there was the Royal Tournament in London.

On 3 March 1985 the Troop was honoured by a visit to St. John's Wood Barracks by the Prince and Princess of Wales. As with all the visitors to the Wood, they were much taken by the size and character of this diminutive little barracks in north London as they were by the horses and soldiers who served there.

Although the show season was diminishing, the 1980s was punctuated with many other events, in particular the number of royal visitors and their interest in the Troop and its role. 1987 was a particularly busy year. On 5 March Her Majesty Queen Elizabeth The Queen Mother carried out her second visit to St. John's Wood and on the 1 June the Troop was on parade in Windsor Great Park for a review by Her Majesty The Queen to mark the 40th anniversary of the naming of the Troop. Over

the next few years, the Queen Mother carried out several other visits to the Wood as indeed did many dignitaries, foreign royalty and military 'Top Brass'.

During the remainder of the decade many improvements and repairs were carried out on the fabric of the new buildings in the barracks and some of the equestrian facilities. The surface in both the riding school and manège were regularly replaced as was that of the perimeter track around the square. The flat-roofed married quarters block at the side of the square had suffered for many years from damp and condensation and one of the remedies was to add a new pitched roof to the structure. The main barrack block was also deteriorating and by 1990 it, too, had a new flat roof covered with felt.

With the collapse of communism and the destruction of the 'Iron Curtain' in 1990, the government of the day began a defence review called 'Options for Change'. By the middle of the decade the armed forces were reduced by almost one third. Fortunately this did not affect those at the Wood too much but the subsequent civilianisation of various services including the guards for the main entrance, did have an impact on the barrack

A splendid collection of trophies from the many military and civilian competitions that Troop personnel had competed in during 1995.

The horses take an inquisitive view of their surroundings on arrival at Rotterdam during one of the many trips to Europe carried out by the Troop during the decade.

Children from a local school show great interest in the work of the Master Saddler during a visit to the barracks in 1995.

The guns prove to be just as interesting!

culture, as did the abolition of the Junior Leaders Regiments. The recruitment of boys into the British Army for employment as trumpeters or drummers had been a tradition that stretched back several hundred years. All this came to an end in 1992. For the King's Troop, who received their trumpeters fully trained from the Junior Leaders Regiment each year, this was an immediate problem, and during the next twenty years they had the difficult task of training soldiers from within the Troop to carry out this duty, which apart from for the sounding of fanfares at shows and displays had, by the turn of the century, almost entirely disappeared.

Perhaps as a result of the ongoing cuts in manpower or maybe just to add something different, the Troop were called upon to provide a team to represent the Army in a Tri-Service Command task competition at the Festival of Remembrance at the Royal Albert Hall in November 1992.

Scenes from the Royal Tournament, 1996.

Left: The second visit of HM The Queen Mother, 1997.

Above: Her Majesty departing from the barracks past the ceremonial gun carriage which carried her late husband King George VI in 1952.

The Troop rank past at Woolwich during the celebrations to mark the bicentenary of the formation of the Royal Horse Artillery in 1793.

It was left to the Navy to design the challenge which was based on the Field Gun Competition at the Royal Tournament. A squad of twelve soldiers under a sergeant was selected and after an intense programme of fitness and technique training they were ready for the first rehearsal. To many people's surprise the Troop team proved to be the strongest and most determined and went on to win almost every run including the final run on the night in front of the Queen, proving to all and sundry that the 'Right of Line' were the best both on and off their horses!

A Royal Salute in Green Park. This is one of the first occasions when Green Park was used for Royal Salutes.

A Royal Salute to mark HM The Queen's Birthday, Hyde Park, 21 April 1997.

Before the Royal Regiment was reduced to the size it is today they were able to celebrate in the summer of 1993, the bicentenary of the formation of the Royal Horse Artillery, at Woolwich, on 1 February 1793. As the saluting battery of Her Majesty's Household Troops, the King's Troop took pride of place in the celebrations and to them came the honour of firing the royal salute for the arrival of Her Majesty and then to lead the Regiment in the march past the Royal dais. The 50th anniversary of the naming of the Troop by King George VI fell on 24 October 1997. This was celebrated with a review by the Queen on Cumberland Green, in Regents Park, the first time for many years that this venue had been used. Fortunately the sun shone and the crowds came out to watch. Among them were several hundred old comrades and many of the married families from St. John's Wood. The format of the parade was a tried and tested procedure: an inspection in Review Order followed by a march

Right: Funeral of Diana, Princess of Wales, 1997. The cortège passes through Horseguards Parade.

Below: The Queen's Birthday Parade, 1999. The Troop formed up in front of the Guards memorial prior to the march past.

Scenes from The Royal Tattoo, 2000, on Horse Guards Parade.

Above: The Troop formed up on the square at the barracks before moving off to fire the Minute Guns for the funeral of HM The Queen Mother, 2002.

Left: At the conclusion of the salute the Troop formed up at Wellington Arch to pay their respects as the hearse and cortège of royal cars pass through on their way to Windsor.

past, a trot past, culminating in the traditional horse artillery gallop past. Thereafter it was the customary march back to barracks via Avenue Road.

The introduction of health and safety legislation and the human rights act in the 1990s had brought other more radical changes to the Troop and the Army as a whole.

One of the changes was the practice of wearing civilian-style hard hats on all mounted duties, instructional rides and exercise, except for when wearing full dress. Another was the abolition of the women's services and the opening up of most of the military occupations previously carried out by men. This included the King's Troop (but not the Household Cavalry). Consequently, from the middle of the decade women were permitted to serve in the Troop. It was during this period that a new tradition began at Christmas time at the Wood when the barracks was opened to local residents and their families on Christmas Eve. This followed after the morning exercise in which a few members of the Troop dressed and decorated with festive flair accompanied the exercise down Norfolk Road.

The increase in traffic in the capital, the changing attitudes and impatience of drivers, and the speed at which everyone seemed to travel, had, by the turn of the 21st century made the morning exercise and the practice of riding one horse and leading two, a positively dangerous affair. Indeed, it was not unusual for a horse to be injured after a collision with an impatient vehicle and its driver.

As the new millennium dawned, life at St. John's Wood Barracks continued with its principal role of ceremonial, though by now there were many other demands upon manpower and resources. The primary saluting bases in London for the past one hundred and fifty years had been St. James's Park and Hyde Park. This changed during the 1990s when Green Park was made available to the Troop during periods of inclement weather which made the use of Hyde Park impractical.

One of the most poignant events of the decade took place in September 1997 when the Troop provided the gun carriage for the funeral of Diana, Princess of Wales.

Immense crowds lined the streets of London as the funeral cortège made its way from Kensington Palace, along Kensington Gardens, down the Mall and through Horse Guards before proceeding down Whitehall on its way to Westminster Abbey. It was perhaps the greatest outpouring of national grief for many years.

The end of the century brought the end of one of the country's most famous military shows: The Royal Tournament, which began in 1880 and at which the saluting battery at the Wood had performed their famous musical drive since 1895. The following year there was a special 'Military Tattoo' on Horse Guards Parade, at which the Troop performed the 'Earls Court' musical drive, but this proved to be a short-lived affair and was never repeated. Occasionally however, there were other military events for the Troop to take part in and during the year

An atmospheric shot of the Troop in action.

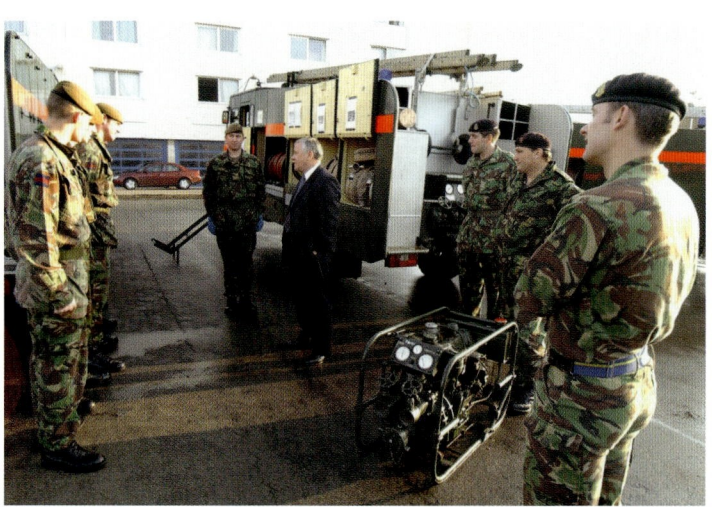

OP FRESCO 2003, the second Firemen's strike. Members of the Troop are briefed on their duties.

they moved to Larkhill for a week or so to perform the musical drive and display at 'Artillery Day', the Royal Artillery's special event on Salisbury Plain.

By any standards, 2002 proved to be one of the busiest years for the saluting battery for a very long time: marked on the one hand by great joy for the celebration of the Queen's Golden Jubilee and much sadness on the death of Her Majesty Queen Elizabeth The Queen Mother, the last 'Queen Empress', on Easter Saturday. The Queen Mother's funeral took the form of a shortened state funeral with her coffin borne on the same gun carriage that had carried her husband, King George VI, fifty years previously. Preceded by the massed pipes and drums of British and Commonwealth armies, the cortège marched in sombre procession from Westminster Hall, where she had lain in state, to Westminster Abbey. The silence of the crowds and the

Above: The second, less formal visit of HRH Princess Anne in 2003. Here she is received at the Officers' Mess by the Regimental Colonel of the Troop and the Commanding Officer.

Right: Princess Anne experiences the work of riding in the gun team.

lament of the pipers were punctuated only by the jingle of harness and the rumble of the gun-wheels. Later that morning the Troop, having completed the Minute Guns, were at Wellington Arch with guns unhooked and barrels dipped as the cortège, with the coffin now carried in a hearse, passed through on its way to Windsor.

A few weeks after this historic event the Troop were at the Royal Windsor Horse Show, which as part of the celebrations for the Queen's Golden Jubilee had been re-titled as the Royal Windsor Tattoo. Later that summer there were further Jubilee celebrations in the centre of London with the Troop firing the gun salute and taking part in the procession through the streets.

During the final decade of their residence at St. John's Wood the Troop carried out all of the normal ceremonial duties with the addition, since 1997, of the Queen's Birthday Parade on Horse Guards, at which the Troop exercised its privilege of leading the Household Troops in the march past the Queen. Although the show season had become depleted

The Director Royal Artillery is conveyed in the Troop 'Dog Cart' to the parade at Regents Park during his inspection, April 2003.

The Queen presents the annual RHA Association trophies to the winning Sub-section after the 60th anniversary parade, Hyde Park

during this period the Troop did succeed in sending individual Gunners across the Atlantic to compete in shows or act as uniformed escorts in at some of the large equestrian events of the time, such as Spruce Meadows in Canada

In 2003 the barracks once again became a temporary fire station when the Firemen's Union called yet another strike. On this occasion however, the timing was selective and although the square was once again used to park Green Goddess fire engines the disruption to both the Troop and the locals was fairly minimal.

On 28 October 2006 there was an Open Day at the Barracks at which more than 600 people, both Troop families and locals attended and they enjoyed a memorable afternoon touring the barracks and watching a display by a gun team on the square. This

60th anniversary parade—Hyde Park, 2007. The Commanding Officer, Major E. L. Bridge RHA reports the Troop ready for inspection.

was the first such Open Day for several years and was greatly popular with everyone. Another important event during a decade punctuated with departures of many kinds was the parade at Woolwich on 26 May 2007—the 291st anniversary of the raising of the Royal Artillery Regiment at Woolwich in 1716— to mark the move from its ancient home. As with many other units and members of the Royal Artillery, the Troop was heavily involved in the event. They performed the musical drive in the afternoon and led the march past at the end of the day. With theatrical timing, the clouds arrived just before the final parade and as the Troop marched past the Master Gunner, the heavens opened and down came the rain!

A new task came in May 2007 when the Troop provided a dismounted guard at Windsor Castle: an unusual duty but one that they performed with their customary style and panache. No sooner had it been completed than they were in Hyde Park for the Troop's 60th Anniversary parade on 28 June 2007. After the parade the Queen was introduced to the officers and senior NCOs and their families as well as many former Commanding Officers of the King's Troop. She also presented the RHA Association annual 'Whips' competition trophy to the champion Sub-section, the first occasion that the trophy had been presented by a reigning monarch.

Planning for the move from St. John's Wood was by now well advanced and several locations were considered, including the old cavalry barracks in Regents Park. Eventually, and with a large twist of irony, it was decided that they would move to the Royal Artillery Barracks at Woolwich, the former home of their forbears, the pre-war Riding Troop.

The Regimental Headquarters of the Royal Artillery moved from Woolwich to their new home at Larkhill on Salisbury Plain by the end of 2007, and on Thursday 12 June 2008, to the sound of a 21-gun salute fired just off the Packway on the old flying field, the new Royal Artillery Barracks at Larkhill was officially opened by the Queen. Larkhill had been the home of the Royal School of Artillery and the principle Royal Artillery training area since before the First World War so the move of the Regimental Headquarters was not as traumatic as might have been expected. All that was now left was for the saluting battery to move from central London to its new home at Woolwich, but before doing so the Troop were honoured by a special valedictory visit.

Christmas at the Wood, 2010—local scenes in Norfolk Road.

To mark the departure of the King's Troop and the Royal Horse Artillery from the Wood, the Queen made her third official visit to the barracks on Friday 24 June 2011. Following a slightly different format from previous visits the Queen toured Right Section Lines and inspected a Section mounted in Full Dress on the Regimental Square. Thereafter she was treated to a short display of Troop training activities in the Riding School before retiring to the Officers' Mess for lunch.

The farewell visit of HM The Queen, 2011.

Top:
Meeting the Troop families.

Bottom:
Inspecting the Troop on the square.

On the last day of occupation, with a heavy dusting of snow decorating the barracks, the King's Troop form up on the regimental square prior to the march-out.

During the summer of 2011 preparations for the exodus to Woolwich gathered pace with several of the married families moving in. Jubilee Buildings, which for more than seventy years had housed many of the families of those who had served at the Wood, were now almost empty. The Senior NCOs married quarters at the side of the square had long since been abandoned and these two buildings, poorly maintained and with a forlorn and unloved air about them, awaited the arrival of the demolition men's hammers. After mounting of the Queen's Life Guard in early September, the process of moving out of the barracks continued. In the meantime, the normal routine of recruit rides and upgrading courses continued until the Christmas break in early December. In early January 2012, the final process of moving to the new stables and barracks at Woolwich began and by the end of the month everything was ready for the Troop's arrival. On 6 February the Troop formed up on the square at the Wood in full dress before marching off to Hyde Park to fire a Royal Salute celebrating the 60th anniversary of the accession to the throne by Her Majesty The Queen. This final march out from the barracks fittingly took place on the day that also marked the death of the King who had granted them their title in 1947.

Once outside the barracks the Commanding Officer and the RSM dismounted, a lone trumpeter sounded the last post, and watched by a large gathering of local residents, school children, old comrades and many hundreds of well wishers, they closed the gates for the last time. Preceded by the Royal Artillery Band the Troop then marched off down St. John's Wood High Street. Thus ended the final chapter in the history of the saluting battery at their ancient home in St. John's Wood.

The Commanding Officer, Major M. G. Edward RHA, leads the King's Troop out of the barracks for the very last time.

Many hundreds of local people and old comrades wave farewell to the Troop as they make their final journey down St. John's Wood High Street on their way to Hyde Park to fire a Royal Salute, 6 February 2012.

St. John's Wood Barracks

Occupants from 1804

Date	Unit	Title in 2012
1804	Corps of Gunner Drivers	Disbanded
1822	Cavalry Riding Establishment	Disbanded
1835	Guards Recruit Depot	Army Training Regiment
1836	Various detachments of Foot Guards	Army Training Regiment
1876	1st Life Guards	Household Cavalry Regiment
1877	Royal Horse Guards	
1878	2nd Life Guards	
1879	1st Life Guards	
1880	A Battery A Brigade Royal Horse Artillery	A Battery (The Chestnut Troop) Royal Horse Artillery
1881	G Battery C Brigade Royal Horse Artillery	132 Battery (The Bengal Rocket Troop) Royal Artillery
1883	C Battery A Brigade Royal Horse Artillery	C Battery Royal Horse Artillery
1886	B Battery B Brigade Royal Horse Artillery	L (Néry) Battery Royal Horse Artillery
1888	B Battery A Brigade Royal Horse Artillery	B Battery Royal Horse Artillery
1889	Barracks vacant	
1891	J Battery Royal Horse Artillery	J (Sidi Rezegh) Battery Royal Horse Artillery
1893	D Battery Royal Horse Artillery	D Battery Royal Horse Artillery
1896	G Battery Royal Horse Artillery	G Parachute Battery (Mercer's Troop) Royal Horse Artillery
1899	Barracks vacant	
1900	V Battery Royal Horse Artillery	V Parachute Battery Royal Horse Artillery
1902	X Battery Royal Horse Artillery	Disbanded
1904	Y Battery Royal Horse Artillery	Disbanded
1906	A Battery (The Chestnut Troop) Royal Horse Artillery	A Battery (The Chestnut Troop) Royal Horse Artillery
1908	BB Battery Royal Horse Artillery	Disbanded
1911	F Battery Royal Horse Artillery	F (Sphinx) Parachute Battery Royal Horse Artillery
1914	L Battery Royal Horse Artillery *(reformed after Néry, September 1914)*	L (Néry) Battery Royal Horse Artillery
1915	B Reserve Brigade Royal Horse Artillery	Disbanded
1919	F Battery Royal Horse Artillery	F (Sphinx) Parachute Battery Royal Horse Artillery
1920	N Battery Royal Horse Artillery	N Battery (The Eagle Troop) Royal Horse Artillery
1923	O Battery Royal Horse Artillery	O Battery (The Rocket Troop) Royal Horse Artillery
1926	M Battery Royal Horse Artillery	M Battery Royal Horse Artillery
1929	J Battery Royal Horse Artillery	J (Sidi Rezegh) Battery Royal Horse Artillery
1932	F (Sphinx) Battery Royal Horse Artillery	F (Sphinx) Parachute Battery Royal Horse Artillery
1936	K Battery Royal Horse Artillery	K (Hondeghem) Battery Royal Artillery
1940	London District Signal Troop	Disbanded
1946	The Riding Troop Royal Horse Artillery	The King's Troop Royal Horse Artillery
1947	The King's Troop Royal Horse Artillery	
1969	Barracks vacated for rebuild	
1972	The King's Troop Royal Horse Artillery	
2012	Barracks vacated	

Index

Acknowledgements

Many people have contributed to the preparation of this book and I would like to acknowledge the assistance I have had from serving and former members of the Royal Regiment of Artillery and others who have answered my letters, given me information and lent me illustrations. In particular I would like to thank the battery commanders of the many Royal Horse Artillery batteries that have served at the Wood; the staff of the Royal Artillery Library, Westminster City Council Archive, the editor and staff of *Gunner* Magazine and the Regimental Journal, the Commanding Officer, the King's Troop Royal Horse Artillery, Colonel J. M. Browell MBE, Major J. C. C. Sworder, Major B. L. Richardson RA, Andrew Knight, Geoffrey Probert, Sergeant Ian Vernon, Anthony Motley, and my clerical assistant Sarah-Jane King.

And finally, special mention must be made of Barbara Cooper, as editor and publishing consultant, and Paul Harding for the design and production.

The book has been produced with financial help or marketing assistance for which I am very grateful from:
Clive and Alison Beecham
Mark Westaway & Son (HorseHage)
The Royal Artillery Institution
The Royal Horse Artillery Association
The Worshipful Company of Farriers
The Society of Master Saddlers

Bibliography

Gunner Magazine—1920–1999
Order of Battle 1914–1918 Part 1
Hance, J.E., Lt. Col.—*Riding Master*
Sworder, John, Maj.—*A short history of St. John's Wood Barracks*
The Royal Artillery Journal—1944
The Royal Artillery Distribution Lists—1880–1939
Wanklyn, Joan—*Guns at the Wood*

Picture Credits

THE HORSES PRAYER

To thee O my master I offer my prayer,
My life and health I give to your safe keeping,
From you I ask only for food and water,
Shelter in winter and summer,
A kind hand and a quiet voice,
Do not use a whip unfairly
Or spur and bit me cruelly,
But give me the understanding
To do your will.
Thus I will serve you cheerfully,
On the long trail and in battle,
In the race and over big fences,
So shall we enjoy our time on earth together.
Enjoy the wind on the hill,
The shadows on the grassland,
The shelter of the trees,
And the warmth of the sun.
Let us know together that companionship
That a horse may give to his master,
And enjoy in this life
God's earth and the fullness thereof.
And when I am old
and have served you well,
Pray, O my master,
Do no sell me to slavery and to a cruel end
But send me to rest with tenderness and kindness
And my gratitude will be your reward,
This I ask in the name of him
who was born in a stable.